THE GREAT LUXURY LINERS

1927-1954

A Photographic Record

William H. Miller, Jr.

Dover Publications, Inc.
New York

TO FRANK O. BRAYNARD
*The world is a better place
because of him*

Published in Canada by General Publishing Company, Ltd., 30 Lesmill
Road, Don Mills, Toronto, Ontario.
Published in the United Kingdom by Constable and Company, Ltd., 10
Orange Street, London WC2H 7EG.

The Great Luxury Liners, 1927–1954: A Photographic Record is a new
work, first published by Dover Publications, Inc., in 1981.

International Standard Book Number: 0-486-24056-8
Library of Congress Catalog Card Number: 80-68054

Manufactured in the United States of America
Dover Publications, Inc.
180 Varick Street
New York, N.Y. 10014

Foreword

As a youngster, I had the wonderful good fortune to be raised in a waterfront town, one directly opposite the great passenger-ship piers of New York City. Those years, the fifties, were marked with as many trips to a shoreside park as I could possibly manage, the newspaper timetables serving as my guide to the comings and goings of splendid ocean liners. At that time there seemed to be more liners than I could ever count. Any given Saturday morning had its own parade: the red-and-black funnels of a French liner, the white hull of a Swedish-American, the billowing flags of one of the Italian queens. The sights were pure magic — man's most characteristic mechanical creations: sleek, powerful and orderly. They had romance and flavor as passengers lined decks as they departed for exotic destinations. And, of course, the personalities of the ships were part of the allure. Some were new, fresh and trend-setting. Others had years behind them — earlier lives, other names, different roles. The elements played their own part, making occasions that were welded into mind and memory: brilliant sunshine glowing on two or three funnels, or a rakish bow emerging out of the fog.

Later, I managed as many presailing visits as was possible. The great ships took on a new dimension. Their innards were vast, magnificent, sometimes fantasy-like. There never seemed to be enough time — three thunderous blasts, clouds of smoke and tiny tugs nosed them out.

Today, that generation of liners is gone, although a link remains in the present breed. Nothing on this planet will ever compare with them.

WILLIAM H. MILLER

Hoboken, New Jersey

Credits

American Export Lines, 114
American President Lines, 87 (top), 143 (top)
Ernest Arroyo Collection, 128 (bottom), 132/133
Belgian Line, 83
Frank O. Braynard Collection, 2–6, 7 (bottom), 8–14, 19, 32/33, 38 (bottom), 39, 42–45, 48/49, 60, 63, 65, 67, 69, 70, 72–74, 75 (bottom), 79, 80 (bottom), 82 (bottom), 87 (bottom), 89–91, 93, 96 (top), 97–99, 103–108, 112, 113, 115 (bottom), 117–120, 122 (bottom), 123, 124 (top), 126/127, 130, 134, 135 (bottom), 140 (bottom), 143 (bottom), 144–146, 150 (bottom), 151–155
Cunard Line, 54, 55, 61, 129
Alex Duncan, 7 (top), 28, 29, 31, 66 (bottom), 86, 121 122 (top), 125, 139
French Line, 16, 21 (right), 22 (bottom), 23 (top), 53 (bottom), 135 (top), 158 (bottom), 159–161
Furness-Bermuda Line, 82 (top)
Hamburg America Line, 15
F. W. Hawks, 75 (top)
Holland-America Line, 138 (top), 156 (top)
Italian Line, 150 (top)
Eric Johnson, 34 (top), 100 (top)

Mariners Museum, 21 (top), 40 (top), 58, 62, 111
Matson Navigation Company, 35
Vincent Messina Collection, 36, 40 (bottom)
Museum of the City of New York (Byron Collection), 17, 18, 20, 22 (top), 23 (bottom), 46, 52, 53 (top), 76/77, 94
Nederland line, 66 (top)
North German Lloyd, 38 (top)
Norwegian America Line, 136
Orient Line, 140 (top), 142
Real Photographs Company, Limited, 81
Schiffsfotos, 92 (top)
Roger Scozzafava, 41, 47, 64 (bottom), 80 (top), 96 (bottom), 100 (bottom), 101, 102
James Sesta Collection, 88
Southern Newspapers Limited, 137
Steamship Historical Society of America, 34 (bottom), 68, 110 (top), 115 (top), 116
Swedish-American Line, 138 (bottom)
Union Castle Line, 30
United States Lines, 25–27, 147–149, 157–161
United States Maritime Commission, 124 (bottom)
World Ship Society, 64 (top), 128 (top), 140

Acknowledgments

Many hands have assisted in the completion of this volume. The author wishes to note the outstanding help, in terms of photographs and information, given by Frank O. Braynard, Vincent Messina, Alex Duncan, Michael Cassar, F. W. Hawks and the World Ship Society Photo Library, Frank Busuttil, the Steamship Historical Society of America, Mariners Museum, Ernest Arroyo, Roger Scozzafava, B. Reeves, Howard Whitford, Clifford Morgan and the United States Lines, William C. North, and Frank Duffy.

Other research materials, bits of important information and patient cooperation came from Norman Walker, Julie Ann Low, James Sesta, Carole Chellis, John Piltzecker and Erwin Abele. Special thanks to Robert Fusco for his careful guidance. Of course, and hardly least, warmest thoughts to my family for their inspiration.

Companies which have assisted in the project include: Adriatica Line, Belgian Line, DFDS Seaways, Finnlines, Holland America Line, Jahre Line, Lion Ferry, P & O Normandy Ferries, Royal Caribbean Cruise Line, Norwegian American Line, Commodore Cruise Lines, Sitmar Cruises, and Captain John Tuanmu of Island Navigation Corporation.

Introduction

For me, one of the lasting pleasures of working on my book *The Only Way to Cross* was meeting others irresistibly drawn to the great ocean liners. One such was Bill Miller, then chairman of World Ship Society's Port of New York Branch. Now, happily for steamer buffs everywhere, he has launched this impeccable treasury of steamers from the last half-century.

He has started, after looking at ships of the twenties, with a turning point in ship design, the *Ile de France* (1927), the French Line's dreamboat. Masked by a conventional profile, passenger spaces were dazzling vistas plucked intact from the Exposition des Arts Décoratifs of 1925. Not a motif, grill or line, not a stick of furniture or meter of fabric was derivative; everything on board was new. Those controversial interiors marked a decorative watershed and most ships that followed in her wake adhered to the same relentless modernity. Tudor, Jacobean, Palladian or Baroque styles, traditional steamship ideals that had dominated ocean-going public rooms since the great sailing steamers, examples of which can be seen in some interior photographs, were hopelessly out of style. The era of the modern liner had begun.

In short order, the *Ile* had four competitors, a pair each from Germany and Italy. Astonishingly resurgent German yards fielded the *Bremen* and the *Europa* — low, rakish racers in the tradition of the turn-of-the-century *Deutschland*. On her maiden voyage the *Bremen* wrested the Blue Ribbon for speed in crossing the Atlantic from the venerable *Mauretania*, the Cunarder which had held it in triumph since 1907. From Genoa and Trieste, the second pair of new ships, the *Rex* and the *Conte di Savoia*, were Mussolini's bid for a share of the Atlantic riches; the *Rex* took the speed prize from the *Bremen*.

New giants were in the offing. The *Normandie* and the *Queen Mary*, the great 1,000-footers, sailed miraculously out of the Depression, vessels of such ponderous dimension that they silenced the statistical one-upmanship of the Western Ocean shipbuilders. In the summer of 1935, the *Normandie* dashed across the Atlantic both ways, faster than any before her. The *Queen Mary*, her cross-channel rival, subsequently shaved hours off the French ship's time, keeping the coveted speed honors until the *United States*, William Francis Gibbs's brainchild, swept the seas forever in 1952.

In September of 1939, the lights of Europe went out. The ships' brilliant upperworks were cloaked in gray. Sailings became furtive — strategic rather than celebratory. As in 1914–1918, the world's liners ensured the swift delivery of tens of thousands of soldier-passengers.

Peace brought a promising surge in shipping. The fifties seem, in fond retrospect, a mid-century evocation of Edwardian extravagance as new tonnage carried millions across the seas. The *Queens* operated in glorious tandem; a white Italian fleet steamed proudly out of the Mediterranean; a flock of Dutch sisters rallied about the prewar *Nieuw Amsterdam;* as the *Liberté*, the ex-German *Europa* assumed the red-and-black funnels of the French Line, joining in lavish service with the revamped, two-funneled *Ile*; the *United States* and *America* carried the stars and stripes on the cold northern run while the *Independence* and *Constitution* offered Yankee alternatives on the southern route. It was a golden decade on all the world's sea lanes, peak years of maritime indulgence.

Then, abruptly, the ships were doomed, cut short by the ominous, ubiquitous shadow of the passenger jet. Even De Gaulle's imperishable gift of the *France* came too late and the inevitable decline began. By the late sixties, irreversible attrition took its toll. Both *Queens* were withdrawn, one to become a California carnival of dubious stability, the other destroyed by a suspicious fire on the eve of a renaissance. The *United States* languishes at her Norfolk pier.

Sadder still was the end of steamship service between Le Havre and New York, between Tilbury and Sydney, between San Francisco and Honolulu. As each ship stopped sailing, there was none to replace her, with the single exception of the *Queen Elizabeth 2*, teethed on adversity and plagued by misfortune, that still carries the colors of a new breed of Cunard cruiseships. Cruising may save the ships, although it seems an uncertain economic area. Leisure sailing, the enjoyment of shipboard life for its own sake, with exotic ports within lazy reach, has spawned new flotillas along the warm-water routes, towering white wedding cakes of ships, floating hotels for a new generation of passengers. One can only hope that these fair-weather clients will find shipboard life as enchanting as their parents and grandparents did.

But if cruising enjoys a vogue, crossing has almost vanished. Links between Old World and New, West and Far East, temperate and tropical, are all aerial now — swift, anonymous and essentially graceless passage between shores. People who yearn for the old way — and I think their number is legion — must turn now to the record. In these haunting pages they should find solace, an evocative look at 25 splendid years. Bill Miller's fleets steam past in glorious review, a golden jubilee retrospective of the world's passenger liners. I have dwelt on the giants, but Miller has seen to it that ships great and small are part of the immortal parade. We are indebted to him for his initiative, scholarship and devotion in assembling this anthology, for remembering so well in a world that finds it too easy to forget.

JOHN MAXTONE-GRAHAM

New City, New York
Christmas, 1980

Contents

THE GREAT
LUXURY LINERS
1927-1954

The Twenties

The twenties were, for the most part, a relatively calm period for ocean liners. The Great War finished, a new armada of ships replaced the casualties. The old colonial trades were reestablished and the mail runs were as important as ever. Britain still had the biggest passenger fleet and reigned over the most prestigious run, the North Atlantic. She had the greatest liners, either by her own design or postwar acquisition. Standing in the forefront were the Cunard and White Star firms, each competing on a weekly transoceanic shuttle. However, with strong determination, the French were moving forward, first with the *Paris* of 1921. In response, Italy shot ahead with its first 30,000 tonners. But, for the most part, size and speed were set aside. American immigration quotas had curtailed traffic requirements. Steerage, the very bloodline of many firms, was sliced. Consequently, new liners were smaller, slower, more comfortable and quaint than luxurious and opulent.

Then, in 1927, the *Ile de France* inaugurated service, becoming the very symbol of the opulence that defined the luxury liner. She created a new dimension in travel, a floating grand hotel rather than a mere commercial ocean-going ferry.

©Hamilton Maxwell, Inc. N.Y.

Ber 150

BERENGARIA.

In the photograph above, Cunard Line's *Berengaria* (foreground) rests at Pier 54, at the foot of West 12th Street, New York City on July 11, 1924. Large, powerful, luxurious, she was one of the Atlantic's prestige boats. The *Berengaria*, the stately *Aquitania* and the illustrious *Mauretania* (then the world's fastest steamship), were known as the "Big Three," carrying thousands of passengers each year between Southampton and New York on a weekly schedule. The service continued even in the North Atlantic's most severe months during the frigid winter. Shown with the *Laconia* (another Cunarder), the *Minnetonka*, the *Homeric*, the *Baltic*, and the *Pittsburgh* beyond her, the *Berengaria* originally was built for the Hamburg-America Line as the *Imperator* and came into service in 1913, on the heels of the *Titanic* disaster. She was ceded to Britain following World War I. [Built by Bremer Vulkan Shipyards, Hamburg, Germany, 1913. 52,226 gross tons; 919 feet long; 98 feet wide; 38-foot draft. Steam turbines geared to quadruple screw. Service speed 23 knots. 2,723 passengers (972 first class, 630 second class, 606 third class, 515 tourist class.]

The sitting room of one of the *Berengaria's* finest suites *(left)* gives an idea of the ship's luxury.

MAURETANIA.

The *Mauretania (above)*, a Cunarder, was one of the most publicized and popular liners ever built. When completed in 1907, she was not only the world's largest passenger ship, but one of the very first to use steam-turbine engines, which were rapidly replacing the older, less efficient steam triple- and quadruple-expansion styles. She also captured the coveted Blue Ribbon in her maiden year and reigned for the following 22 years as the fastest ocean liner on the Atlantic, a distinction which doubtless brought her additional passengers. The trophy was finally snatched, in the summer of 1929, by Germany's new *Bremen*. Like most major liners built prior to the First World War, the *Mauretania* was a coal burner. This meant that she was often seen belching huge amounts of heavy, dark smoke, and that below deck some 200 stokers — known with something of a fearful reverence as the "black gang" — worked in almost inferno-like conditions coaling the long string of furnaces. By the early twenties, however, oil-fired systems had come into practical use. Immediately, the changeover eliminated those 200 additional crewman, improved maintenance and overall efficiency and dispensed with the bothersome process of loading coal. Beginning in the summer of 1921, the *Mauretania* spent eight months at her builder's yard and was converted to oil firing. The process eventually affected every major liner on the Atlantic. [Built by Swan, Hunter & Wigham Richardson Shipbuilders Limited, Newcastle, England, 1907. 30,696 gross tons; 790 feet long; 88 feet wide. Steam turbines geared to quadruple screw. Service speed 25 knots. 1,756 passengers after 1921 (589 first class, 400 second class, 767 third class.]

The magnificence and splendor of the *Mauretania's* interior is apparent in the views shown overleaf.

The *Mauretania*. The first-class lounge *(opposite)* featured classical columns and a glass dome. The main dining room *(above)* was two decks high with a center well. The sports deck aft *(below)* was equipped for various games.

ALAUNIA.

Although Cunard operated some of the largest and most elegant liners, company directors envisioned a more relaxed trend developing on the Atlantic during the twenties. Consequently, there appeared a near assembly line of 14,000–20,000 tonners which traded both to the United States and eastern Canada. These ships, such as the *Alaunia (opposite, top)*, managed 15 knots, creating an 8–10 day Atlantic crossing from Britain. [Built by John Brown & Company Limited, Clydebank, Scotland, 1925. 14,030 gross tons; 538 feet long; 65 feet wide; 30-foot draft. Steam turbines geared to twin screw. Service speed 15 knots. 1,706 passengers (484 first class, 1,222 third class).]

In 1928 photographs were taken of a better third-class cabin *(opposite, bottom)* and the first-class main lounge *(above)*.

HOMERIC.

White Star's *Homeric (opposite)*, the largest twin-screw liner in the world during the twenties, gained the reputation as one of the steadiest ships on the North Atlantic in a period long before stabilizers (antirolling devices). [Built by Schichau Shipyards, Danzig, Germany, 1913–22. 34,351 gross tons; 774 feet long; 82 feet wide; 36-foot draft. Steam triple-expansion engines geared to twin screw. Service speed 19 knots. 2,766 passengers (529 first class, 487 second class, 1,750 third class).]

The view above catches two youngsters racing their tricycles on the boat deck.

MAJESTIC.

White Star Line's *Majestic (above)* was the largest passenger liner afloat in the twenties. She had been designed and nearly completed by the Germans as the *Bismarck*, but was ceded to Britain following World War I. Her size, prestige and luxurious interiors made her one of the most popular and profitable liners on the North Atlantic prior to the Depression. At the end of the decade, she had the particular distinction of being the first liner to show motion pictures with sound. Also operating the four-stack *Olympic* and the medium-sized *Homeric*, White Star provided weekly sailings between New York and Southampton, in direct competition with Britain's ocean liner giant, Cunard. The 56,551-ton *Majestic* had two "near sisters" — the 59,900-ton *Leviathan* of United States Lines and the 52,200-ton Cunarder *Berengaria*. The *Majestic's* tonnage was registered according to British standards while *Leviathan*, seemingly larger at 59,900 was listed under United States regulations, the American standard making ships larger in comparison to those of Britain. Consequently, London's scales left *Leviathan* at a much lighter 48,000 tons. This was an era of furious competition when national prestige was re-

flected in the liners and "biggest," "longest," "fastest" and "most luxurious" could mean the difference between profit and failure. [*Majestic:* Built by Blohm & Voss Shipbuilders, Hamburg, Germany, 1922. 56,551 gross tons; 956 feet long; 100 feet wide; 38-foot draft. Steam turbines geared to quadruple screw. Service speed 23.5 knots. 2,145 passengers (750 first class, 545 second class, 850 third class).]

Speaking of passengers similar to those shown here (*opposite, top*), one *Majestic* passenger wrote to a friend named Franklin Delano Roosevelt: "If you are a lover of the seas and ships that sail them then the *Majestic* is nothing more than a gorgeous hotel filled with the usual obnoxious crowd. The same average case reigns in the second as in the first class, the difference being solely a matter of dollars, certainly not habits. As the steward will tell you, the best class of people travel second class at third class rates." But the harsh judgment could not have applied to the youngsters enjoying a birthday on board the ship in 1928 (*opposite, bottom*), nor did it prevent crewmembers, stevedores and dry-dock workers from affectionately referring to her as the "Magic Stick."

LEVIATHAN.

The *Leviathan (above)* was originally the German *Vaterland*, seized at New York in the First World War. Following the Armistice, she underwent a refurbishing at Newport News, Virginia, one that kept her off the Atlantic until her maiden voyage for United States Lines on July 4, 1923. Her career was marked by financial problems, the lack of a suitable running mate within the company, American prohibition laws that kept her "dry," and a common theory of the day that British and European liners were more glamorous, luxurious and gave better service. The *Leviathan* was a far cry from an ordinary passenger ship. Her indoor pool, for example, known as the Roman Bath, was 65 feet long and done in tile, marble and bronze. There were supporting pillars, fountain cascades and upper-level spectator galleries. Her restaurant was managed by the famed Ritz Carlton Company. The line showed passengers "pre-release talkies" in the lounge. [Built by Blohm & Voss Shipbuilders, Hamburg, Germany, 1914. 59,956 gross tons (48,932 by British measurements); 950 feet long; 100 feet wide; 38-foot draft. Steam turbines geared to a quadruple screw. Service speed 23 knots. 3,008 passengers (940 first class, 666 tourist class, 1,402 third class).]

Notable *Leviathan* passengers shown on the opposite page included Rudolph Valentino *(top left)*, Gertrude Hoffman *(top right)*, Pola Negri *(bottom left)* and a pet leopard with its unidentified mistress *(bottom right)*.

The *Leviathan*. The bedroom and sitting area in a first-class cabin.

HAMBURG.

Following the First World War, the great Hamburg-America Line was all but depleted of passenger-ship tonnage. Rebuilding began as soon as possible; their first new liner was ready by 1923. The *Hamburg* — a product of 1926 — presented a very traditional profile: upright funnels with a slight rake and lifeboats in double tiers in rather historic quadrant davits. Furthermore, she was typical of the large passenger ship with a substantial cargo capacity, in this case with six holds. [Built by Blohm & Voss Shipbuilders, Hamburg, Germany, 1926. 21,691 gross tons; 635 feet long; 72 feet wide. Steam turbines geared to twin screw. Service speed 19 knots. 1,150 passengers (222 first class, 472 second class, 456 third class).]

Two ocean giants in port together—the FRANCE and PARIS at New York

French L

FRANCE.

The four-funnel *France* (left in the photo above) sits alongside the larger *Paris* at the French Line's 15th Street terminal in New York. [*France:* Built by Chantiers de l'Atlantique Shipyard, St. Nazaire, France, 1912. 23,769 gross tons; 713 feet long; 75 feet wide; 35-foot draft. Steam turbines geared to quadruple screw. Service speed 23 knots. 1,623 passengers (517 first class, 444 second class, 510 third class, 152 steerage).]

The *France*, one of the most popular liners on the trans-

atlantic run and certainly one of the most lavish ever built, was known with affection as the "Chateau of the Atlantic." Her decor throughout was opulent Louis XIV. However, her most unusual feature was the introduction of the grand staircase at sea. This sweeping arrangement in the ship's first-class dining room (*opposite*) provided the passengers with dramatic entrances and developed such appeal that it became a highlight of many major liners built in the twenties and thirties.

PARIS.

French Line ships had enormous appeal in the twenties — "floating bits of France itself," as one brochure aptly stated. Service and accommodations were fine but the cuisine was its most outstanding feature. It is said that more sea gulls followed the *Paris (above)* than any other ship in hopes of grabbing scraps of the *haute cuisine* that were dumped overboard. [Built by Chantiers de l'Atlantique, St. Nazaire, France, 1921. 34,569 gross tons; 764 feet long; 85 feet wide. 1,930 passengers (560 first class, 530 second class, 840 third class).]

The grand staircase aboard the *Paris (opposite)* descended to the foyer. The ceilings were done in glass extending into a dome. The French Line embodied a continuing stress on modernity, made obvious by a comparison of the dining room aboard the *France* of 1912 to the style which appeared a mere nine years later.

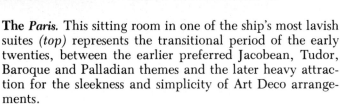

The *Paris*. This sitting room in one of the ship's most lavish suites *(top)* represents the transitional period of the early twenties, between the earlier preferred Jacobean, Tudor, Baroque and Palladian themes and the later heavy attraction for the sleekness and simplicity of Art Deco arrangements.

The wireless office *(bottom, left)* often witnessed some of the voyage's most exciting moments and tending it made great demand on the attendant officers as messages were relayed between ship and shore, often in an almost endless procession. A traveling Hollywood starlet or industrial tycoon might receive hundreds of cables during the course of a week's crossing and might dispatch an equal number.

There were other occasions of more serious nature: distress calls from foundering freighters or for injured crewmen on other vessels needing the services of the liner's doctor.

The oil-fired turbine emerged during the twenties, replacing the prewar coal system and allowing tidy, near-polished perfection in the engine rooms *(bottom, right)*. Finally, interested passengers — who were very often the gentlemen aboard — could be invited below decks by the chief engineer for a tour of the machinery. The very core of the ship's energy system impressed these onlookers, such as that on board the *Paris*, where the 34,000-ton liner could be driven at 21 knots with over 2,500 souls hardly feeling the effort.

ILE DE FRANCE.

In 1926, the French Line released an elaborate gold-covered booklet devoted entirely to the company's new flagship, seen above at sea. The illustrations depicted huge, ornate yet modern public rooms, women passengers carrying feather fans and smoking cigarettes, and borzois being led around the sun deck. The ship's degree of modernity was unlike anything previously seen. The dining room was spectacular. There were also a chapel, a shooting gallery, an elaborate gymnasium and even a merry-go-round for the younger passengers. Every cabin had beds instead of bunks. [Built by Chantiers de l'Atlantique, St. Nazaire, France, 1927. 43,153 gross tons; 791 feet long; 91 feet wide; 34-foot draft. Steam turbines geared to quadruple screw. Service speed 23.5 knots. 1,786 passengers (537 first class, 603 second class, 646 third class).]

At sailing time, the three-deck-high main foyer (right), with its grand staircase, was filled with elegantly dressed passengers, their well-wishers, company officials and possibly some reporters. Chatter and laughter filled the air as did cigarette smoke and the sound of popping champagne corks. Bellboys scurried in their glistening uniforms, delivering bon voyage telegrams and shiny baskets of fruit. Then, suddenly, a rattle passed through the ship. A mighty blast on the Ile's whistle meant that departure was thirty minutes off.

S. S. ILE de FRANCE   MAIN FOYER AND GRAND STAIRCASE   French Line

The *Ile de France*. The first-class dining room *(above)*. The first-class salon *(below)*.

The *Ile de France.* Two first-class suites de luxe.

S. S. ILE de FRANCE   THE BOAT DECK
First Class   French Line

The *Ile de France*. Passengers in first class, such as those strolling on the boat deck *(above)*, enjoyed a new, sleek luxury. The great first-class dining room aboard the *Ile de France* towered three decks. Never before had the traveling public seen a room of such massive simplicity yet startling attractiveness. It was a design based not on some landside theme, but created for this ship itself in complete originality. The era of the "ocean liner style" had begun. Some cabins, although equally modern, still had exposed steel ceilings. When portholes were opened, the sound of the sea filled the room. A maid would assist madame, filling the closets and arranging the dressing tables. Perfumes and cosmetics made their way to the separate bathroom. The gentleman would have the valet press his suits and evening clothes. The great steamer trunks were unloaded and sent off to a storage room for the remainder of the trip.

Even many of the chairs aboard the *Ile de France* were totally new in design. As each of the major liner companies subsequently planned their next passenger ships, one of the first steps was to visit this most exquisite, extraordinary and trend-setting French vessel.

PRESIDENT ROOSEVELT.

The great liners were not the only means of making a crossing during the twenties. "Cabin liners" were quite typical. Cabin class dominated these ships in terms of shipboard space if not in numbers. They also had third-class accommodations. United States Lines' *President Roosevelt (above)* was a fine example of this type. She worked between New York, the Channel ports and Bremen. [Built by New York Shipbuilding Corporation, Camden, New Jersey, 1922. 13,869 gross tons; 535 feet long; 65 feet wide. Steam turbines geared to twin screw. Service speed 17 knots. 437 passengers (201 cabin class, 236 third class).]

The *President Roosevelt*. The cabin-class dining room *(opposite)* boasted a stained-glass arc-ceiling and plank-like flooring. Cabin-class stateroom No. 117 *(above)* reveals the ship's unpretentious comfort.

SCANSTATES (above).
Combination passenger-cargo ships became popular, comfortable modes of transport during the twenties. Some travelers preferred them to the faster glamor queens on the main runs. American Scantic Line's *Scanstates* sailed between New York and Scandinavian ports. The firm was a division of the well-known Moore-McCormack Lines. [Built by American International Shipbuilding Corporation, Hog Island, Pennsylvania, 1919. 5,163 gross tons; 390 feet long; 54 feet wide. Steam turbines geared to a single screw. Service speed 13 knots. 90 cabin-class passengers.]

EDAM (opposite, top).
The Holland-America Line was known as the "Spotless Fleet." Its ships ranged from the 28,000-ton *Statendam* to smaller, combination passenger-cargo vessels such as *Edam*. *Edam's* work was divided: Rotterdam to New York and Baltimore, or farther afield to Havana and Veracruz. [Built by de Schelde Shipyards, Flushing, Holland, 1921. 8,871 gross tons; 466 feet long; 58 feet wide. Steam turbines geared to a single screw. Service speed 13 knots. 974 passengers (174 first class, 800 third class.]

LALANDIA (opposite, bottom).
Lalandia, of Denmark's East Asiatic Company, was one of a series of combination passenger-cargo ships that had a novelty: no traditional funnel. Exhausts were expelled through a pipe system in the third of the four masts. She and her running-mates sailed from Copenhagen out to the Orient via the Mediterranean, through Suez and along the East. [Built by Nakskov Shipyard Limited, Nakskov, Denmark, 1927. 5,146 gross tons; 405 feet long; 53 feet wide; 24-foot draft. Burmeister and Wain diesels geared to twin screw. Service speed 13 knots. 29 first-class passengers.]

LLANGIBBY CASTLE *(above).*
The foremost firm on the African runs was Britain's Union Castle Line, which had an elaborate mail-ship service between Southampton and the Cape. Among the many ships on that service was *Llangibby Castle*, a classic example of twenties "motorship modern" — squat funnels against a rigid profile. [Built by Harland and Wolff Limited, Govan, Scotland, 1929. 11,951 gross tons; 507 feet long; 66 feet wide. Burmeister & Wain type diesels geared to twin screw. Service speed 14.5 knots. 450 passengers (250 first class, 200 third class).]

MULBERA *(opposite, top).*
British India Line connected the eastern section of the Empire. *Mulbera* was one of six sister ships that sailed between London and Calcutta via the Suez Canal. Although otherwise unnotable, she was selected to carry the Duke and Duchess of York (later King George VI and Queen Elizabeth) out to East Africa in the mid-twenties; not until the fifties did British royalty use aircraft for overseas tours. [Built by Alexander Stephen & Sons Limited, Glasgow, Scotland, 1922. 9,100 gross tons; 466 feet long; 60 feet wide. Steam turbines geared to twin screw. Service speed 13 knots. 170 one-class passengers.]

LECONTE DE LISLE *(opposite, bottom).*
Messageries Maritimes of Marseilles had the *Leconte de Lisle* on the route to Saigon, then a French colonial stronghold. During that era such ships had lounges and decks filled with high commissioners with their entourages and families, servicemen, engineers, traders and civil servants going off for a tour of duty in the colonies. [Built by Société Provençale de Construction, La Ciotat, France, 1922. 9,877 gross tons; 452 feet long; 61 feet wide. Steam turbines geared to twin screw. Service speed 15 knots. 240 passengers in five classes.]

LANCASTRIA.

Charter sailings and pleasure cruises were becoming more popular in the late twenties. Each winter, for example, the Cunard Line ran a four-month cruise around the world. In addition, there were sailings to the Caribbean, around South America and Africa, to the Mediterranean and Black Seas, and in the summer to the North Cape, Scandinavia, western Europe, eastern Canada and short trips to Bermuda, Nassau and Havana. Fares for the 1929 world cruise started at $900. Here Cunard's *Lancastria* departs on a special American Legion sailing in the spring of 1928, from New York to London. [Built by William Beardmore & Company Limited, Glasgow, Scotland, 1922. 16,243 gross tons; 578 feet long; 70 feet wide; 30-foot draft. Steam turbines geared to twin screw. Service speed 16.5 knots. 1,846 passengers (235 first class, 355 second class, 1,256 third class).]

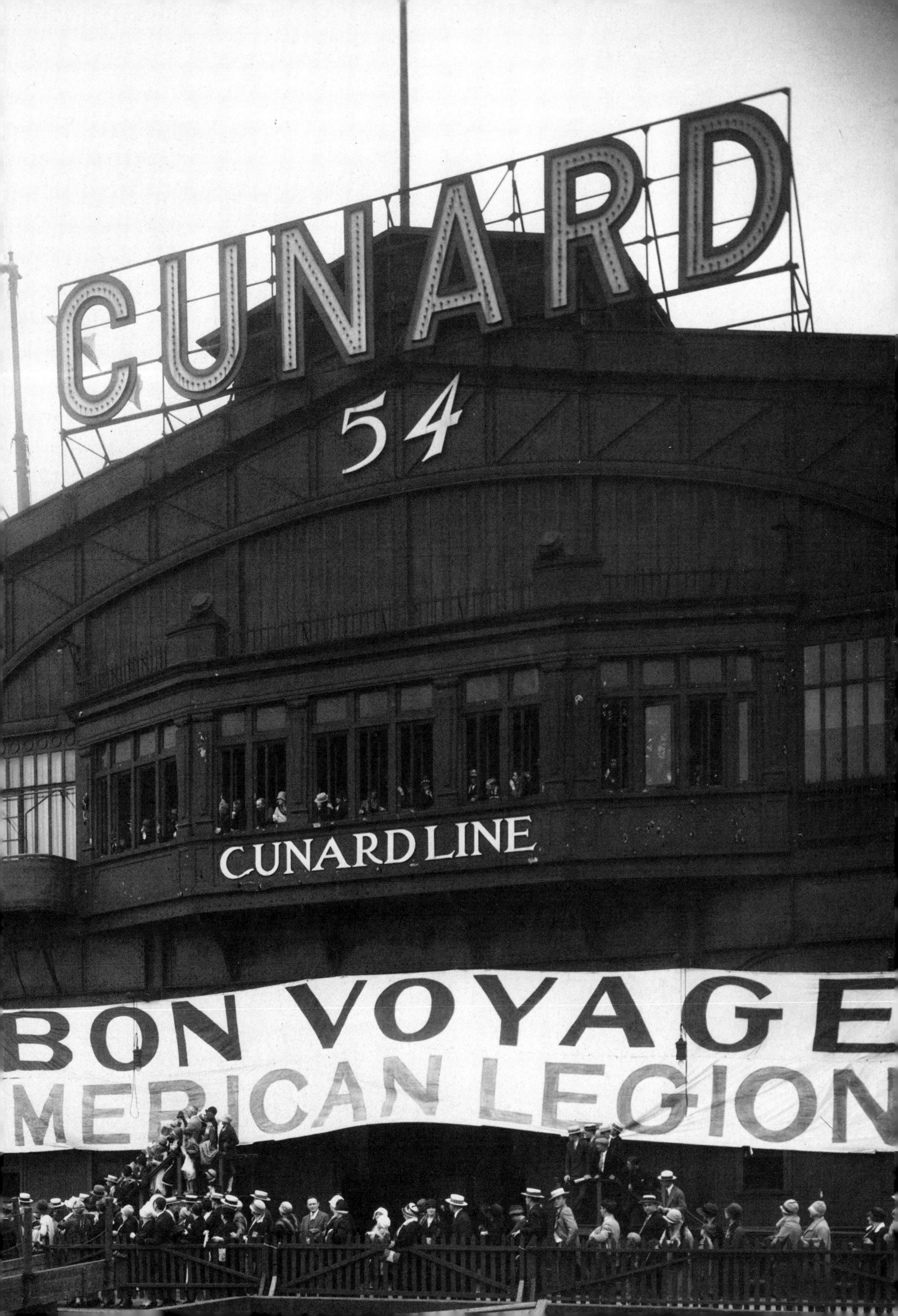
CUNARD
54
CUNARD LINE
BON VOYAGE
MERICAN LEGION

SANTA BARBARA (opposite, top).
The Grace Line of New York was commanded by the *Santa Barbara*, shown here, and her sister ship, the *Santa Maria*. They traded to the Caribbean carrying port-to-port passengers as well as round-trip cruise travelers. These ships are among the very few American-registry liners that were built abroad. [Built by Furness Shipbuilding Company, Haverton-on-Tees, England, 1928. 8,060 gross tons; 486 feet long; 64 feet wide. Diesels geared to twin screw. Service speed 16.5 knots. 150 first-class passengers.]

BERMUDA (opposite, bottom).
The Furness-Bermuda Line's New York–Bermuda holiday trade with older, smaller ships was so successful that it built the luxurious *Bermuda* in 1927. Initially, the ship was intended to have Bermuda sailings only during the winter and longer cruises for the remainder of the year. However, immediate response was so great that the Bermuda run became a year-round operation. [Built by Workman, Clark & Company Limited, Belfast, Northern Ireland, 1927. 19,086 gross tons; 547 feet long; 74 feet wide. Doxford-type diesels geared to quadruple screw. Service speed 17 knots. 691 passengers (616 first class, 75 second class).]

MALOLO (above).
Matson Navigation Company of San Francisco did much to develop tourism in the Hawaiian Islands. In 1927, it commissioned its largest ship, the *Malolo* (later rechristened the *Matsonia*, as shown), for first-class luxury service between San Francisco, Los Angeles and Honolulu. Suddenly, opulence had spread to the Pacific. The *Malolo* and later Matson liners advertised superb public rooms, spacious cabins, swimming pools, a gymnasium, and a staff, including a hairdresser, to provide superlative service. The *Malolo* introduced new, vastly improved safety standards which especially influenced all subsequent American passenger liners. During her trial runs in the western Atlantic, she collided with a Norwegian freighter with an impact equal to that which sent the *Titanic* to the bottom 15 years earlier. Strides in compartmentation allowed the *Malolo* to survive and sail into New York harbor flooded with over 7,000 tons of sea water. [Built by William Cramp Shipbuilders, Philadelphia, Pennsylvania, 1927. 17,232 gross tons; 582 feet long; 82 feet wide. Steam turbines geared to twin screw. Service speed 21 knots. 693 first-class passengers.]

STELLA POLARIS.

One of the most classic cruise ships ever built, the *Stella Polaris* was delivered to Norway's Bergen Line in 1927. Styled after a millionaire-class luxury yacht, the *Stella* had space for a mere 165 passengers. During the summers, she cruised along the fjords, to the North Cape and Spitzbergen and into the Baltic. In spring and autumn, there were voyages around the Mediterranean; for winter, a luxurious circumnavigation of the globe. [Built by Gotaverken Shipyards, Gothenburg, Sweden, 1927. 5,209 gross tons; 416 feet long; 51 feet wide; 17-foot draft. Burmeister & Wain diesels geared to twin screw. Service speed 15 knots. 165 first class passengers.]

The Giants

The *Ile de France* was the first of the "floating luxury hotels," but hardly the last. No sooner had she been finished in 1927 when drawing boards were turned toward a new select group — bigger, faster, more lavish than any yet seen. Their accommodations were the publicity man's dreams come true — from carpeted kennels with running water in the *Conte di Savoia* to white grand pianos in the *Normandie's* finest suites. All of these giant ships were beyond the financial scope of even the greatest firm. Fortunately, governments were generous with loans, for national prestige rested in the technology and magnificence of the ships.

The biggest rivalry was over the Blue Ribbon for the fastest transatlantic crossing. Britain's *Mauretania* held it for 22 years; in 1929 it passed to Germany's *Bremen*. The Italian *Rex* took it in 1933; France's *Normandie* won it two years later. By 1938, the glory went back to Britain, firmly secured by the *Queen Mary*.

Sadly, however, none of the giants — with the exception of the *Queen Mary* — earned a profit. Apart from the staggering construction, maintenance and fuel costs, other factors worked against them. The *Bremen* and the *Europa* attracted fewer passengers than expected, victims of anti-German and then anti-Nazi feelings. The *Empress of Britain* was too large for either the Canadian or world-cruise trades. The "Sunny Southern Route" of the *Rex* and the *Conte di Savoia* never had the lure of the supposedly more plush northern run. Finally, the *Normandie* — probably the most magnificent and surely the most innovative — inhibited many potential passengers by her very luxury. In four years of transatlantic crossings, she rarely sailed more than half-full.

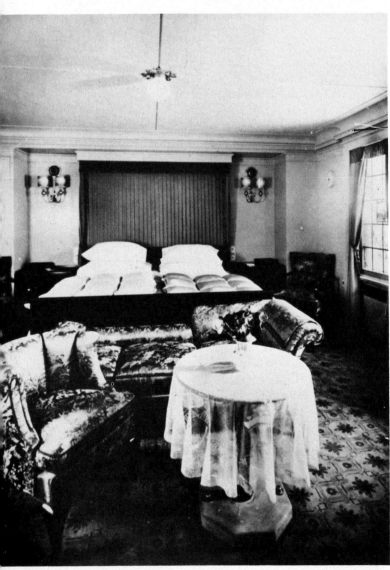

EUROPA.

Germany's resurgence following the First World War was incredible. Nearly depleted of ships in 1918, there were two 50,000-tonners on the building ways a decade later: the *Bremen* and the *Europa (above)*. They appeared on the drawing boards in the mid-twenties at 35,000 tons, 700 feet long. Then, shortly after keel laying, ideas changed. Their length jumped to over 900 feet and machinery and accommodations went in to make them the fastest, most luxurious liners on the Atlantic. North German Lloyd's publicity department decided on an extravagant introduction: the two liners crossing together on their maiden voyages as they *both* captured the Blue Ribbon from Britain's *Mauretania*. The two ships were launched one day apart in August 1928. Then the ambitious scheme went astray. While being fitted out at Hamburg the following spring, the *Europa* was swept by a fire which destroyed most of her interior. Repairs took another full year. Consequently the *Bremen* — still adhering to the original timetable — sailed alone to New York. Her record, in July 1929, stood at 4 days, 17 hours. She had captured the Blue Ribbon. [*Europa*: built by Blohm & Voss Shipbuilders, Hamburg, Germany, 1930. 49,746 gross tons; 936 feet long; 102 feet wide. Steam turbines geared to quadruple screw. Service speed 27 knots. 2,024 passengers (687 first class, 524 second class, 306 tourist class, 507 third class).]

The decor of a first-class cabin *(left)* reflects the German taste of the period.

The *Europa.* The main dining room *(above)* and the ballroom *(below)*.

BREMEN.

The engineering world marveled at the new *Bremen* in her maiden summer of 1929. Aside from her enormous propelling machinery, she introduced the use of the bulbous bow, a knife-like stem that substantially reduced drag. The *Europa* took the Ribbon from her sister in 1930 by a very slight increase in speed. But the *Bremen* proved the faster and regained the title shortly thereafter until the honors were finally taken by Italy's *Rex* in 1933. The *Bremen*, having slightly more prestige than the *Europa*, also proved to be more popular than her sister ship. Originally the pair had low, squat funnels, which gave them a particularly sleek appearance. But smoke and soot often gathered on the aft passenger decks so the funnels were doubled in height.

[*Bremen*: A/G Weser Shipbuilders, Bremen, Germany, 1929. 51,656 gross tons; 938 feet long; 102 feet wide. Steam turbines geared to quadruple screw. Service speed 27 knots. 2,200 passengers (800 first class, 500 second class, 300 tourist class, 600 third class).]

North German Lloyd publicists continued to work hard at keeping the German sisters in the news. Early in their careers a seaplane resting in a catapult was placed between the two funnels of each ship. Thirty-six hours before the ship docked the mails were sent ahead by air *(below)*. The scheme succeeded for a time, but in the end proved costly and awkward. By 1935, the technique was dropped.

EMPRESS OF BRITAIN.

In 1928, Canadian Pacific ordered a luxury liner for their Atlantic service to Quebec City, hoping to lure Americans from the Middle West and West away from the traditional patterns of sailing out of New York. She was launched as the *Empress of Britain* on June 11, 1930 when, for the first time, ceremonies were broadcast by radio to Canada and the United States. After her maiden trip, the novelty wore off and in the end her northerly service could not compete with the shorter, more glamorous crossings from Manhattan on more fashionable ships. The designers of the *Empress of Britain* provided carefully for around-the-world winter cruises and each January until 1939 (except 1933) she sailed from New York on a 30,000-mile, 128-day globe-circling journey. For this trip, the two outer screws were shipped inboard to save drag and reduce fuel costs. The route was traditional: east through the Mediterranean and Suez to India, Java, Bali, China, Japan, the American West Coast and back to New York via Panama. The *Empress* held the records for size for transit of the Suez and Panama Canals until they passed to the *Bremen* in the thirties. The fare for these cruises was no trifle. Minimum was $2,100, and a suite could cost $16,000. Servants went for $1,750 extra. However, the cruises operated in the red; the *Empress of Britain*

was one of the least profitable liners of her time. Her proudest moment probably came in 1939, when she brought King George VI and Queen Elizabeth home to England after a goodwill tour of North America in June. The royal couple and their entourage occupied a string of suites for the crossing. [Built by John Brown & Company Limited, Clydebank, Scotland, 1931. 42,348 gross tons; 758 feet long; 97 feet wide. Steam turbines geared to quadruple screw. Service speed 24 knots. 1,195 passengers (465 first class, 260 tourist class, 470 third class).]

The *Empress of Britain's* Mayfair Lounge was inspired by ancient Greek architecture. Rich walnut complemented by modern designs of silver were used for wall paneling. The columns and pilasters were of scagliola. The vault overhead was done in panels of amber glass, each one bearing a golden sunburst while at the intersection of the ribs were the signs of the zodiac in bas-relief.

Rich woods from the British Empire decorated the sitting rooms of the apartments de luxe.

The first-class gymnasium featured electric horses, rowing and bicycling machines, punch bags, medicine balls and "automatic camels."

The *Empress of Britain*. The Mayfair Lounge *(opposite)*. An apartment de luxe *(above)*. The first-class gymnasium *(below)*.

REX.

Amid great competition from other steamship companies, the Italian Line carried out a very attractive and enthusiastic publicity campaign for its two largest liners, the *Rex* and the *Conte di Savoia.* Both ships were dubbed "the Riviera afloat." To carry the theme even further, sand was scattered around the outdoor swimming pools, creating a beach-like effect highlighted by multicolored umbrellas. The first of this pair to be completed was, appropriately, the largest and the fastest. It was christened the *Rex* in August 1931, in the presence of the King and Queen of Italy. In her goal of a record-breaking maiden trip, her first run was a dismal failure. She sailed from Genoa in September 1932, after a send-off from Premier Mussolini, with a passenger list of international celebrities. Unfortunately, while approaching Gibralter, serious mechanical difficulties arose. Repairs took three days. Half her passengers requested to leave. Further complications arose on the Atlantic; lengthy repairs were required in New York before returning to Europe. The *Rex* finally captured the Blue Ribbon in August 1933, an honor held for two years before passing it on to the *Normandie.* [Built by Ansaldo Shipyards, Genoa, Italy, 1932. 51,062 gross tons; 880 feet long; 96 feet wide. Steam turbines geared to quadruple screw. Service speed 28 knots. 2,258 passengers (604 first class, 378 second class, 410 tourist class, 366 third class).]

The *Rex*. The lido deck was the largest yet seen on a transatlantic liner.

CONTE DI SAVOIA.

No less popular or extravagant than the *Rex*, although not a record-breaker, the *Conte di Savoia* carried off most of her maiden trip in November 1932 without event until, 900 miles off the American coast, an outlet valve below the waterline jammed and blew a sizable hole in the hull. In a matter of minutes, the huge ship's dynamo compartment was flooded with seawater. After inspection it was computed that she might sink within five to eight hours. For-tunately, due to the superhuman labors of the crew and engineers, temporary repair efforts succeeded in plugging the hole with cement. [Built by Cantieri Riuniti dell'Adria-tico, Trieste, Italy, 1932. 48,502 gross tons; 814 feet long; 96 feet wide. Steam turbines geared to quadruple screw. Ser-vice speed of 27 knots. 2,200 passengers (500 first class, 366 second class, 412 tourist class, 922 third class).]

NORMANDIE.

The *Normandie (left)* was the world's most glamorous ship of the thirties. The $60 million she cost to build, a figure not easily matched in the decade between the wars, was underwritten heavily by the French government. Novelty and extravagance were the keynotes of her design. The famed Penhoet shipyards, the builders of the *Ile de France*, were commissioned, along with the finest designers, decorators, sculptors, engineers and specialty technicians in Europe. A former designer of the Czar's warships, Vladimir Yourkevitch, was placed in charge. The ship was originally known as the "super-*Ile de France*" and the French Line gradually released each alluring detail: the first liner to exceed 1,000 feet in length, the first to surpass 60,000 tons. (The comparison with a four-masted schooner below gives some idea of her size.) The same Paris offices were overwhelmed with suggestions for names: the *Neptune*, the *Lindbergh*, the *Pershing*, the *President Doumer*, the *Jeanne d'Arc*, the *Napoleon*, the *Benjamin Franklin* and even the *Maurice Chevalier*. The world's largest bottle of champagne — six quarts in all — was used by Madame Lebrun, the First Lady of France, to christen the ship *Normandie* at the launch on October 29, 1932. A ton of soap and more of suet and lard were used to grease the launching ways. Even at that, 100 workmen were swept into the Loire River by the backwash. A victim of the Depression, the big liner was laid up for a time at her fitting-up dock. Her maiden trip was postponed until May 1935. [Built by Chantiers de l'Atlantique, St. Nazaire, France, 1935. 82,799 gross tons; 1,028 feet long; 117 feet wide. Steam turboelectric engines geared to quadruple screw. Service speed 29 knots. 1,972 passengers (848 first class, 670 tourist class, 454 third class).]

On her maiden crossing, the *Normandie* averaged 32 knots and broke all records. Her time: 4 days, 3 hours, 14 minutes. The Italians sadly relinquished the Blue Ribbon held by the *Rex*. Berlin Radio announced that "true" speed of the *Bremen* and *Europa* would soon be shown, retaking the honor. The British calmly reported that the *Normandie* would probably crack in half on her return sailing. Seen overleaf are *half* the crew of the great liner, about 675 figures, ranging from officers and department chiefs to gardeners and bellhops.

The *Normandie*. The first-class restaurant *(opposite, top)* was slightly larger than the Hall of Mirrors at Versailles. Surely one of the most outstanding rooms ever put to sea, it was a superb creation of Lalique fixtures, hammered bronze and glass. Other details were equally mind-boggling: the restaurant measured 300 feet in length, rose three decks and seated 1,000. The indoor pool was 80 feet long with a graduated depth. The theater seated 380 on two levels. The chapel comfortably held a 100 total. The garage held 100 cars. There were large foyers, private drawing rooms, bars, a grill room, terrace café, writing rooms, libraries, a shooting gallery, a novelty shop, a bank, clothing store, gymnasium and special restaurants for children and servants. The Winter Garden boasted fresh greenery, fountain and caged birds. Doormen outside the main restaurant wore powdered wigs.

The great bronze twin doors to the Grand Hall *(opposite, bottom)* were removed during the early years of World War II and eventually found their way to Our Lady of Lebanon Church in Brooklyn Heights, New York.

Beautiful Dupas glass panels covered the walls in the Main Lounge *(above)* and specially created Aubusson tapestries were used for chair upholstery.

The ship's tourist-class accommodations, such as the Grand Salon *(below)*, were outstanding compared to most other liners of the period.

QUEEN MARY.

Before they merged in 1934, Cunard and White Star were each planning a superliner. Cunard ordered an 80,000-tonner from Clydebank, Scotland. White Star had a 60,000-ton motorship in mind that would come from Harland and Wolff at Belfast, but the company's unhealthy financial state was further complicated by the Great Depression and their "dream ship" was abandoned. Cunard's liner survived, despite periodic and sometimes lengthy delays at the shipbuilders. Her name was kept a tight secret at first. Staggering statistics floated out of the Cunard Liverpool headquarters. Simultaneously, across the Channel, France's *Normandie* was under construction. The race between the two was on before either was launched. Queen Mary traveled to the Clyde in September 1934 to give the liner her name. It was the first christening by a British monarch, and marked as the Queen's first public speech in her 24 years as consort. The new *Queen Mary* emerged in the spring of 1936, a year after the *Normandie*. She was less modern than her rival. Instead, Cunard had built a stately looking ship with less pretentious interiors. [Built by John Brown & Company Limited, Clydebank, Scotland, 1936. 81,235 gross tons; 1,018 feet long; 118 feet wide. Steam turbines geared to quadruple screw. Service speed 29 knots. 2,139 passengers (776 first class, 784 tourist class, 579 third class).]

The Queen Mary. Splendor and majesty are clearly evident in the first-class main lounge. On her sixth Atlantic crossing, in the summer of 1936, the *Mary* took the Blue Ribbon from the *Normandie*. After a hard-pressed battle, the *Normandie* regained the title in 1937. Another year passed before the *Queen* recaptured the prized pennant with a run of 3 days, 21 hours, at a speed of nearly 31 knots. The rivalries between the two superships were not restricted to speed. Other publicity figures were just as desireable. In 1935, the *Nor-*

mandie had a gross tonnage of just over 79,000. She was the biggest in the world. A year later, the *Mary* was placed at 81,000. Not to be outdone, the *Normandie* had a large deckhouse built on one of her aft decks, which pushed her tonnage to 83,000. Such were the national and corporate rivalries of the era.

On the vast expanse of the boat deck *(over)* passengers promenaded during idle moments.

FIVE GIANTS.
Occasionally the world's largest liners were docked together between sailings to and from Europe. Seen in this March 1937 view, taken in New York, are (from left to right) the *Europa*, the *Rex*, the *Normandie*, the *Georgic* and the *Berengaria*.

The Depression

These were the leanest years for every passenger-ship firm. Their very life-blood — the voyager — disappeared in vast numbers. Over a million passengers had crossed the Atlantic in 1929. By 1935, the figure had dropped by more than half.

Although the greatest giants were built during these very years, sponsored by government monies, liners struggled for their very existence. Some were sent cruising — sometimes less than half full. It was a preferable alternative to mothballs or, far worse, the scrapheap. Others were less fortunate, such as the classic case of the Atlantic Transport Line's *Minnetonka*, a 21,000 tonner junked on her tenth birthday in 1934.

Most of the older Atlantic queens went and — with the exception of the *Aquitania* — the four-stacker disappeared. Near the end, each underwent slow, painful stripping. Stained-glass windows, sofas, mantelpieces, even washbasins, were auctioned off — sometimes to nostalgic fans. Then the empty hulls went off to the scrappers.

DEPRESSION RUNS.

Cunard's regal *Mauretania (above)*, the Blue Ribbon holder for 22 years, was repainted white in the early thirties and sent on weekend "cruises to nowhere," escapist voyages out to sea. There were also trips to Havana and Nassau, Port-au-Prince and Bermuda. Six days to Nassau in 1934 cost $70.

Another Cunarder, the *Berengaria (opposite)*, was in equally serious trouble: hard times killed off her profits, her aging structure left her prey to small fires and staff cutbacks made her seem almost shabby. She turned to Depression cruising—overnight "booze cruises" that overcame American Prohibition, weekends at sea, jaunts along the East Coast to Nova Scotia and occasional runs to Bermuda and the Caribbean. The prices were low and right for the day. Those who remembered her in the palmier Atlantic era now referred to her as the "Bargain-area."

SCRAPPING.

The dismantling process often presented some horrifying scenes. In this case, aboard the *Berengaria* in 1938 at the breakers in Scotland, the former main ballroom and some staterooms have been reduced to rubble. The promenade and boat decks are cluttered with debris and the forward funnel has been sent crashing down.

OLYMPIC.
The great ships desperately sought income during the Depression. Cunard-White Star's *Olympic*, resting in the floating dock at Southampton during her annual overhaul, made one-day Bank-Holiday cruises. [Built by Harland & Wolff Limited, Belfast, Northern Ireland, 1911. 46,439 tons, 882 feet long; 92 feet wide. Steam triple expansion engines geared to triple screw. Service speed 21 knots. 1,447 passengers in 1932. (618 first class, 447 tourist class, 382 third class).]

THE TREND TOWARD CRUISING.

What remained of the regular liner trades at this time had to struggle to survive. The Italian Government created the Italian Line from three Atlantic companies in 1932. North German Lloyd and Hamburg America merged their sailings as Hapag-Lloyd. Cunard joined with the financially ailing White Star Line in 1934. Immediately following the union, Cunard-White Star sent eight liners — including the mammoth *Majestic* and the *Olympic* — to the boneyards.

The White Star *Doric (above, top)* was also pulled off the North Atlantic in the early thirties. Revamped as a cruising liner, she made some voyages to the Mediterranean, the Canary Islands, Scandinavia and the Caribbean. She was sold for scrap in 1935 after only 12 years service. [Built by Harland & Wolff Limited, Belfast, Northern Ireland, 1923. 16,484 gross tons; 601 feet long; 68 feet wide; 31-foot draft.

Steam turbines geared to twin screw. Service speed 16 knots. 2,300 passengers (600 cabin class, 1,700 third class).]

The *Roma* of the Italian Line *(above, bottom)* set sail from New York in 1935 on a 58-day Mediterranean cruise. With fares beginning at $340, she went to Madeira, Cadiz, Tangier, Malaga, Algiers, Palma de Majorca, Cannes, Malta, Port Said, Haifa, Beirut, Rhodes, the Dardanelles (advertised as "passage by daylight"), Istanbul, the Bosporus, Piraeus, Corfu, Kotor, Dubrovnik, Venice, Messina, Naples, Monaco, Southampton, Boulogne-sur-Mer and Rotterdam before returning to New York. [Built by Ansaldo Shipyards, Genoa, Italy, 1926. 32,583 gross tons; 709 feet long; 82 feet wide. Steam turbines geared to quadruple screw. Service speed, 22 knots. 1,675 passengers (375 first class, 600 second class, 700 third class).]

PARIS.

The brilliant acclaim for her kitchens did not keep the luxurious *Paris* from sailing a third full in the early thirties. The French Line avoided the possibility of "lay-up" by pressing the ship into cruise work. To some, it seemed scandalous to have such ships lazily roaming the Mediterranean or Scandinavia with a mere 300 millionaires on board.

EFFECTS OF THE SLUMP.

Even combination passenger-cargo ships on the Amsterdam-to-Indonesia run were hard hit. The Nederland Line was resourceful in sending the *Tarakan (opposite, top)* on "youth cruises" from Holland to the Norwegian fjordlands. As many as 600 teenage boys traveled in specially created dormitories for as little as 25 Dutch guilders. [Built by Wilton-Fijenoord Shipyards, Rotterdam, Holland, 1930. 8,183 gross tons; 469 feet long; 62 feet wide; 32-foot draft. M.A.N. diesel geared to single screw. Service speed 14.5 knots. 21 passengers.]

The number of ships declined even further during the Depression as many of the older liners reached their normal and mandatory retirements. These older ships generally required more repairs and maintenance, and therefore more money. Union Castle's 30-year-old *Walmer Castle (oppo-*

site, bottom) went her way in 1932. Among her passengers had been Rudyard Kipling. [Built by Harland & Wolff Limited, Belfast, Northern Ireland, 1902. 12,546 gross tons; 576 feet long; 74 feet wide. Steam quadruple-expansion turbines geared to twin screw. Service speed 17.5 knots. 754 passengers (336 first class, 174 second class, 244 third class).]

The *Majestic (above)* docked at Southampton for the last time in March 1936. Two months later she was sold to British shipbreakers for a mere £115,000. Her masts were cut down, funnels shortened and lifeboats stripped. Then came a brief reprieve. At the scrapper's she was sold to the Admiralty and became the permanently moored training ship H.M.S. *Caledonia.* Unfortunately, she was swept by fire in 1939 and was then quickly dismantled for the war effort.

LEVIATHAN.

The end of the United States Lines' *Leviathan* was one of the saddest of all, a slow death that took nearly four years. She finished her last commercial trip in September 1934 and, docked at Hoboken, turned into a ghost ship—lifeboats gone, funnels capped, silent innards, lonely vigils by watch-men. Few foresaw another great war coming, when she could have been invaluable as a trooper. Her owners abandoned any hope for revival. Numerous tugs yanked the dinosaur from her slip in the winter of 1938, and she crossed to a Scotland scrapyard with a skeleton crew.

BELGENLAND.

The Red Star Line's *Belgenland* — renamed *Columbia* in her last year — was a favorite cruiseship of the late twenties and early thirties. But then the gaiety and loyal following were suddenly gone. Even cheap "booze cruises" failed. On May 4, 1936, she was deliberately run aground at the scrapping yard and invaded by a small army of torch-bearers. In itself, the task provided jobs for the junking crews. [Built by Harland & Wolff Limited, Belfast, Northern Ireland, 1914–1917. 24,578 gross tons; 697 feet long; 78 feet wide. Steam triple expansion turbines geared to triple screw. Service speed 17 knots. 2,600 passengers (500 first class, 600 second class, 1,500 third class).]

PILSUDSKI.

Poland's Gdynia America Line was in great need of new tonnage by the thirties, but could do nothing without sufficient cash reserves. A novel solution developed: Poland gave Italy five years worth of coal shipments in return for two 14,000-ton passenger ships. The new ships—the *Piłsudski* (above) and her sister *Batory*—had materials and equipment that came from no less than a dozen countries. Affectionately they were dubbed the "international ships." Kitchen utensils, kettles, fire-fighting gear and gyrocompasses came from the United States. The anchors, laundry machines and refrigerating plants were from Denmark. Czechoslovakia furnished the iron used in the hull; England provided the steering gear, boilers and propellors; Scotland contributed the distilling plants; the bow and stern portions were delivered by Hungary; sheets of plating came from Austria; the lifeboat davits and switchboards from Germany; and the fuel pumps and engine parts from Switzerland. [Built by Cantieri Riuniti dell'Adriatico, Monfalcone, Italy, 1935. 14,294 gross tons; 526 feet long; 70 feet wide. Sulzer diesels geared to twin screw. Service speed 18 knots. 759 passengers (355 tourist class, 404 third class).]

Colonies,
Cruising and the Mails

In spite of the Depression some shipowners actually managed to add new liners while others somehow kept their existing fleets intact.

The new ships tended to be medium-sized. On the Atlantic they were more economical and could be pushed into cruising quite easily. In other trades, they came into being largely to serve the vast colonial empires. These ships were vital links for administrative personnel and their families, the military, traders and — just as important — for the uninterrupted flow of cargo and mail to and from the motherland. Quite comfortable and adequate, these ships had little need for great size and speed.

Cruise ships — again in the medium-size range — grew in importance, possibly because of the escapism they provided from world conditions. However, few of them were pure cruise in nature. They also catered to port-to-port passengers and were fitted with profitable, if not large, freight spaces. In some instances further support came from mail contracts.

The mails were a justifiable reason, at the time, for the very being of a passenger ship. Freighters were able to handle this precious cargo but were all too often much slower. Therefore, many liners, although not greatly profitable in the thirties, survived as a result of their combined passenger and cargo roles, world politics and a lack of aircraft competition. Quite simply, for many trips a ship literally provided the *only* way to go.

BRITANNIC.

Despite the slump in the thirties, some North Atlantic ship-lines actually developed a fine new class of medium-sized liners, often referred to as the "mailships." White Star Line's *Britannic (above)* came out of Belfast in May 1930. Designed for the Liverpool–New York service, she and her sistership *Georgic* (1932) were great examples of motorliners of the day: flat funnels (the forward one was a dummy housing wireless equipment) and low superstructures that created a long, slender silhouette. [Built by Harland & Wolff Limited, Belfast, Northern Ireland, 1930. 26,943 gross tons; 712 feet long; 82 feet wide. Burmeister & Wain

diesels geared to twin screw. Service speed 18 knots. 1,553 passengers (504 first class, 551 tourist class, 498 third class).]

The main restaurant in the *Britannic's* sister ship *Georgic (opposite, top)* was two decks high in the center, had indirect ceiling lights and a large three-paneled mirror at the entrance.

The first class indoor promenade aboard the *Georgic (opposite, bottom)* boasted flowered-print armchairs and sofas set against a modern carpet. The upright "trumpet" light fixtures on the right were common to many passenger ships during the thirties.

The *Britannic*. The bedroom of a first-class suite, 1930.

WASHINGTON.

The *Washington* (above) and her sistership the *Manhattan* were built for the United States Lines' run to the Channel ports and Hamburg. They had the simple well-balanced profile of two masts and two funnels, a concept best seen later in Cunard's *Queen Elizabeth*. [*Washington*: New York Shipbuilding Company, Camden, New Jersey, 1933. 24,289 gross tons; 705 feet long; 86 feet wide. Steam turbines geared to twin screw. Service speed 20 knots. 1,130 passengers (580 cabin class, 400 tourist class, 150 third class).]

The officers of the *Washington* underwent periodic examinations on the bridge. In the case below, the use of the sextant was being checked.

The *Washington.* Although the overall decor of the ship was intended to be sleekly modern, the smoking room returned to an earlier style that included carved woodwork, heavier-looking furniture, a center skylight and the stuffed heads of a moose, deer and bison. The room was obviously a male preserve.

77

LANCASTRIA (above).

Cunard's *Lancastria* met with some brisk weather as she headed out to sea in the autumn of 1937. During the thirties, her owners had the largest fleet on the Atlantic and one of the most extensive. Passenger services were run from London, Southampton, Liverpool, Belfast, Glasgow, Cobh as well as across the English Channel, from Le Havre, Cherbourg and even more distant Hamburg. Cunarders called at New York, Boston, Halifax, St. John's, Quebec City and Montreal. In itself, Cunard was a small empire.

CALAMARES (opposite, top).

The United Fruit Company's combination passenger-cargo liners, such as the *Calamares*, were known as "the Great White Fleet." It was made of a vast assortment of attractive ships, all with hulls painted a crisp white, that carried about 100 passengers each on two- and three-week voyages to Central and South America and the Caribbean. The points of departure varied: New York, Boston, Baltimore, even New Orleans. In this age before mass aircraft holidays, the ships provided the grandest and most comprehensive excursions to romantic, far-off lands. [Built by Workman, Clark and Company, Belfast, Northern Ireland, 1913. 7,782 gross tons; 470 feet long; 55 feet wide. Steam quadruple ex-

pansion engines geared to twin screw. Service speed 15 knots. 143 first-class passengers.]

SANTA PAULA (opposite, bottom).

Passenger-ship sailings out of New York during the thirties sometimes ran to as many as eight or ten per day, frequently providing parades for lunchtime viewers on the Manhattan shore. In this aerial photograph, there were three noontime departures: *Santa Lucia* (bottom) was bound for a cruise around South America; *President Harrison* (top, left) was off on a four-month trip around the world; and *Santa Paula* (top, right) went for two weeks in the Caribbean. *Santa Paula* was one of four sister ships built for the Grace Line's runs to the Indies and South America both from New York and San Francisco. The design balance rested between the 300 passengers and about 7,000 tons of cargo. The accommodations were of high standard and included a well-appreciated tropical novelty: a roll-back ceiling over the restaurant which was located between the twin funnels, allowing passengers to dine under the stars. [Built by Federal Shipbuilding and Drydock Company, Kearny, New Jersey, 1932. 9,135 gross tons; 508 feet long; 72 feet wide. Steam turbines geared to twin screw. Service speed 19 knots. 300 passengers (240 first class, 60 second class).]

ORIENTE *(opposite).*

The Ward Line's *Oriente* sailed every other week from New York on seven-day cruises to Havana, then one of the Caribbean's most popular ports-of-call. The ship was a great favorite of honeymooners since minimum fares began at $75. [Built by Newport News Shipbuilding and Drydock Company, Newport News, Virginia, 1930. 11,520 gross tons; 508 feet long; 70 feet wide. Turboelectric engines geared to twin screw. Service speed 20 knots. 530 passengers (430 first class, 100 tourist class).]

Permanently fitted outdoor swimming pools were coming into their own by the thirties. Aboard the *Oriente (bottom)* there were side benches and tables covered by multicolored umbrellas. There was luncheon on deck, cocktails before dinner and dancing under a night sky.

ALCANTARA *(above).*

Services to South America from British and European ports were quite sizeable during the thirties. First-class passengers used the ships for business and holiday. However, just as on the North Atlantic, the greatest revenues came from those in third class, the immigrants, who were seeking new lives or escaping oppression. Homebound, the profits were made in transporting the vast quantities of Argentine beef in the freezer compartments. Britain's *Alcantara* of the Royal Mail Lines was one of the mightiest and fastest on the Latin-American circuit. With her sister *Asturias*, she provided monthly sailings from Southampton via Cherbourg and Lisbon to Rio de Janeiro, Santos, Montevideo and Buenos Aires. At the end, there was a two-week layover, making it the ideal cruise for at least a few of her first-class passengers. [Built by Harland & Wolff Limited, Belfast, Northern Ireland, 1927. 22,909 gross tons; 666 feet long; 78 feet wide. Steam turbines geared to twin screw. Service speed 18 knots. 1,319 passengers (331 first class, 220 second class, 768 third class).]

MONARCH OF BERMUDA and QUEEN OF BERMUDA (opposite).

The *Monarch of Bermuda* and the *Queen of Bermuda (top)* berthed together in the harbor of Hamilton, Bermuda. Deluxe by world standards of the time, they became known as the "millionaire's ships." Every passenger cabin was fitted with a private toilet and full bath or shower, quite a precedent for the early thirties. At times these sisterships—so marvelously popular—carried as many as 4,500 passengers every three weeks on cruises to Bermuda. [*Monarch of Bermuda:* Built by Vickers-Armstrongs Shipbuilders Limited, Newcastle, England, 1931. 22,424 gross tons; 579 feet long; 76 feet wide. Steam turboelectric engines geared to quadruple screw. Service speed 19 knots. 830 passengers (799 first class, 31 second class). *Queen of Bermuda:* Built by Vickers-Armstrongs Shipbuilders Limited, Newcastle, England, 1933. 22,575 gross tons; 580 feet long; 76 feet wide. Steam turboelectric engines geared to quadruple screw. Service speed 19 knots. 731 passengers (700 first class, 31 second class).]

The two-deck-high main lounge of the *Queen of Bermuda (bottom)* was done in polished woods with slight metallic balances, and with a stage at the far end. White ducts for the ventilation system are located on the trims.

ALBERTVILLE (above).

The Belgian Line's *Albertville* was in service to the colonies, sailing from Antwerp to ports in the Congo. [Built by Ateliers et Chantiers de la Loire, St. Nazaire, France, 1928. 11,047 gross tons; 521 feet long; 62 feet wide. Diesels geared to twin screw. Service speed 16.5 knots. 400 passengers in three classes.]

IROQUOIS *(opposite).*
The American liner *Iroquois* of the Clyde Mallory Lines made winter runs between New York and Miami, Jacksonville and Havana and summer sailings to Maine and Nova Scotia. [Built by Newport News Shipbuilding and Drydock Company, Newport News, Virginia, 1927. 6,209 gross tons; 409 feet long; 62 feet wide; 21-foot draft. Steam turbines geared to twin screw. Service speed 18 knots. 600 passengers.]

STRATHMORE *(above).*
P & O Steam Navigation's *Strathmore*, launched in August 1935, was noteworthy as one of the biggest liners ever built for the "Down Under" trade. The P & O and Orient lines were quite separate firms in the thirties but both dominated the Australian service. Together, over 20 liners sailed from London or Southampton to Fremantle, Brisbane, Melbourne and Sydney. Their ships were of two types. The larger breed, generally in excess of 20,000 tons, handled the normal passenger business. The second group, smaller, slower and usually older, worked the immigrant line with vast numbers in a single, steerage-like setting. [Built by Vickers-Armstrongs Shipbuilders Limited, Barrow-in-Furness, England, 1935. 23,428 gross tons; 665 feet long; 82 feet wide. Steam turbines geared to twin screw. Service speed 20 knots. 1,110 passengers (445 first class, 665 tourist class).]

KARANJA *(above)*.

British India Line's *Karanja* ran a local run, shuttling out of Indian ports. Colonial administrators and servicemen and their families filled the upper deck quarters. Below, over 1,000 "deck passengers" used her for resettlement voyages, pilgrimages, even remote work projects. [Built by Alexander Stephen & Sons Limited, Glasgow, Scotland, 1931. 9,890 gross tons; 486 feet long; 64 feet wide. Steam turbines geared to twin screw. Service speed 18 knots. 1,350 passengers (250 saloon class, 1,100 third class).]

PRESIDENT HOOVER *(opposite)*.

The *President Hoover (top)* and her sistership the *President Coolidge* of American President Lines carried the Stars and Stripes on the transpacific trade from San Francisco, touching at Yokohama, Hong Kong, Manila and Shanghai. [Built by Newport News Shipbuilding and Drydock Company, Newport News, Virginia, 1931. 21,936 gross tons; 654 feet long; 81 feet wide. Steam turboelectric engines geared to twin screw. Service speed 20 knots. 988 passengers (307 first class, 133 tourist class, 170 third class, 378 steerage).]

The ship featured an elegant and spacious first-class main lounge *(bottom)*.

MILWAUKEE (*opposite*).

In 1935, after some time on the transatlantic route, Hamburg America Line's *Milwaukee* was repainted white and was restyled as a floating health spa. [Built by Blohm & Voss Shipbuilders, Hamburg, Germany, 1929. 16,754 gross tons; 575 feet long; 72 feet long. M.A.N. diesels geared to twin screw. Service speed 16.5 knots. 559 first-class passengers.]

HAZARDS AT SEA.

Mishap on a summer cruise (*above*). The *Iroquois*, on a trip out of New York, ran aground in a dense fog at Bald Porcupine Island, Maine, on July 14, 1936. Several hundred passengers and crew had to be sent ashore in small boats—a dramatic way of starting a summer vacation.

In December 1937, following a frigid Atlantic crossing, crewmen chipped away at chunks of ice aboard the Polish liner *Piłsudski* (*right*).

Not all pleasure cruising was pleasure. Returning from a holiday run with over 500 passengers and crew aboard, Ward Line's *Morro Castle* (*over*) caught fire on September 8, 1934. Although she was only a few hours steaming time south of New York harbor and a mere six miles off the Jersey coast, incompetence and chaos turned the situation into disaster. She was abandoned, all too late, after claiming 133 casualties. Tides brought the blistering hulk to the shoreline of resort Asbury Park, where a horrifying impression was made on the thousands of spectators who gathered in morbid curiosity. After a thorough investigation of the tragedy, more stringent safety standards were instituted for American passenger ships. [Built by Newport News Shipbuilding and Drydock Company, Newport News, Virginia, 1930. 11,520 gross tons; 508 feet long; 70 feet wide. Steam turboelectric engines geared to twin screw. Service speed 20 knots. 530 passengers (430 first class, 100 tourist class).]

MONTE SARMIENTO (*above*).

In the mid-thirties the Nazi propaganda machine ran "Strength through Joy" cruises — political indoctrination sessions aboard a variety of German liners under the guise of holiday trips along the Norwegian coast or into the Baltic. Hamburg-South America Line's *Monte Sarmiento*, dressed in swastika banners, carried as many as 1,500 per trip. [Built by Blohm & Voss Shipbuilders, Hamburg, Germany, 1924. 13,625 gross tons; 524 feet long; 66 feet wide. M.A.N. diesels geared to twin screw. Service speed 14 knots. 2,470 passengers (1,328 third class, 1,142 steerage).]

NIEUW AMSTERDAM (*opposite*).

The Holland America Line had sufficient cash reserves to build a large national flagship, the biggest ever to be constructed in Holland. Queen Wilhelmina named her the *Nieuw Amsterdam* in the spring of 1937. Proudly, she was dubbed the Dutch "Ship of Peace," since there were absolutely no provisions for possible war use incorporated in her design. When she crossed to New York for the first time, in May 1938, the owners of the *Nieuw Amsterdam* could hardly ignore the frightening strength of neighboring Nazi Germany. [Built by the Rotterdam Drydock Company, Rotterdam, Holland, 1938. 36,287 gross tons; 758 feet long; 88 feet wide. Steam turbines geared to twin screw. Service speed 20.5 knots. 1,220 passengers (556 first class, 455 tourist class, 209 third class).]

The *Nieuw Amsterdam*. The liner was Holland's "ship of state," just as the *Normandie* was France's and the *Queen Mary* was Britain's. Numerous Dutch artists vied for the honor of creating some part of the ship, which was to be light-colored and spacious. Her owners proclaimed her "the ship of tomorrow," and consequently, in some obvious ways, such as the sitting room in the Surinam Suite, she was the most modern European liner of the thirties.

1939

Although this was an uneasy year, with war machines building in Europe and the Far East, ocean-liner business continued. The *Bremen* and the *Europa* worked just as before, if only guarded a bit more heavily while in New York. The *Normandie* cruised to Rio for Carnival in February, and the *Empress of Britain*, as usual, went around the world for four months.

New liners were coming out of the yards at a faster rate than any time since the twenties. American, British, French, Dutch, Swedish, German and even Japanese lines were building or ordering brand-new flagships for routes throughout the world. Then, suddenly, on September 1, it all collapsed.

Almost all liner services ceased and commercial trade, if only temporarily, was shunted aside. Shipyards were hard pressed to convert liners quickly to transports and troopers.

Many ships — particularly the giant class — sat out the end of this year in safety. The neutral ships, such as America's, worked at evacuation. Their capacities more than tripled, they were filled with thousands of fortunate souls able to escape the threatening, fast-moving enemy armies.

THE APPROACH OF WAR.

The Nazi banner flies at the bow of the *Europa (opposite, top)* in the summer of 1939.

The 51,000-ton *Bremen (opposite, bottom)* passed through the Panama Canal during her winter South American cruise in 1939, establishing a record for transit size and emphasizing German might. This record by a passenger liner was not altered until, nearly 35 years later, the 66,000-ton *Queen Elizabeth 2* outranked her German predecessor.

In June the Hamburg America liner *St. Louis* drifted off Havana *(above)* carrying 915 Jewish refugees from Nazi Germany who were barred from entering the island. Friends and relatives could only wave from shore. Small boats with Cuban police and soldiers surrounded the ship to pick up possible suicides. The ship was forced to sail from Cuban waters and returned to Europe. [Built by Bremer Vulkan Shipyards, Vegesack, Germany, 1929. 16,732 gross tons; 574 feet long; 72 feet wide. M.A.N. diesels geared to twin screw. Service speed 16 knots. 973 passengers (270 cabin class, 287 tourist class, 416 third class).]

DESTRUCTION OF THE *PARIS*.
The *Normandie* was temporarily trapped in drydock at Le Havre as the *Paris* (right) burned on April 18 and then quickly capsized. She was one of the nearly a dozen French-owned passenger ships which had been destroyed by fires within a decade.

SPECIAL N.Y. WORLD FAIR CRUISE

GEORGIC *(opposite, top).*
Meanwhile, much of the world continued to ignore the dark clouds on the horizon. Cunard-White Star sent the stately *Georgic* on a four-day Fourth of July weekend cruise from New York to Halifax — escapism for $45. [Built by Harland & Wolff Limited, Belfast, Northern Ireland, 1932. 27,759 gross tons; 711 feet long; 82 feet wide. Burmeister & Wain diesels geared to twin screw. Service speed 18 knots. 1,542 passengers (479 cabin class, 557 tourist class, 506 third class).]

MAURETANIA *(opposite, bottom).*
Cunard's second *Mauretania* was given a maiden reception at New York in June, but after several round trips, she was repainted gray and took on gun mountings. Her capacity quickly jumped from 1,360 passengers to 7,124 troops. [Built by Cammell Laird Shipbuilders Limited, Birkenhead, England, 1939. 35,738 gross tons; 772 feet long; 89 feet wide. Steam turbines geared to twin screw. Service speed 23 knots. 1,360 passengers (440 cabin class, 450 tourist class, 470 third class).]

COLOMBIE *(above).*
French Line's *Colombie*, normally on the Le Havre–West Indies run, made a special cruise to New York and the World's Fair in that fateful summer. [Built by Ateliers et Chantiers de France, Dunkirk, France, 1931. 13,391 gross tons; 509 feet long; 66 feet wide. Steam turbine geared to twin screw. Service speed 16 knots. 491 passengers (201 first class, 146 second class, 144 third class).]

COLUMBUS.

On August 24, with the political situation in grave uncertainty, the *Europa* headed for New York with a full load of passengers. While still off European shores, Berlin ordered her to return immediately. Blacked out and with radio silence, she reversed course and dumped her worried passengers back on the Bremerhaven docks. Another North German Lloyd liner, the *Columbus*, was on a Caribbean cruise at the time. She unloaded her American passengers at Havana and darted to neutral Veracruz. In December, Hitler suggested a quick trip home to Germany. The poorly planned voyage ended when she was deliberately scuttled by her crew to avoid capture some 300 miles off the Virginia coast. [Built by Schichau Shipyards, Danzig, Germany, 1922. 32,581 gross tons; 775 feet long; 83 feet wide; 36-foot draft. Steam turbines geared to twin screw. Service speed 23 knots. 1,724 passengers (479 cabin class, 644 tourist class, 602 third class).]

THE LAST SAILING OF THE *BREMEN*.

The *Bremen* was at New York on August 30, less than two days before the peace-breaking invasion of Poland. She had been detained deliberately by American authorities, who were fearful that munitions might go abroad in her. However, American neutrality and political pressures permitted her to sail that evening, without passengers. Her 900 crew members gave the Nazi salute as she passed the Statue of Liberty. Some expected a speedy, direct trip to Bremer-haven, no matter how risky. Instead, she was repainted in gray camouflage while at sea. She wandered far north to Iceland and finally to Murmansk. Briefly, she hoistered the Soviet flag as a precaution. Then she worked her way slowly along the Norwegian coast, hiding in fogbanks and clinging close to the shoreline. Nearly four months later, on December 10, she docked at Bremerhaven — never to sail again. She was destroyed by fire at her pier in March 1941.

THE SINKING OF THE *ATHENIA* *(opposite)*.
The British-flag Donaldson liner *Athenia* was the first casualty of the war. On September 3, 200 miles west of the Hebrides, she was torpedoed and sunk by a Nazi U-boat with the loss of 112 lives. The news was horrifying. War had begun on the high seas. [Built by Fairfield Shipbuilding and Engineering Company, Glasgow, Scotland, 1923. 13,465 gross tons; 538 feet long; 66 feet wide. Steam turbines geared to twin screw. Service speed 15 knots. 1,552 passengers (314 cabin class, 310 tourist class, 928 third class).]

TRANSPORTING REFUGEES *(above)*.
Their anxiety ended, European refugees wave to friends on the pier as the *Iroquois* docks in New York on October 11.

Having been warned by the German Admiralty that she would meet the *Athenia's* fate in the Atlantic waters, the ship was met at sea by destroyers and a Coast Guard vessel and was escorted into the harbor.

COMMERCIAL CROSSINGS CEASE *(over)*.
A photograph of New York's West Side luxury liner piers in the fall of 1939 reflects the unusual, tense situation. Cunard's *Aquitania* was already repainted in wartime gray. Across the slip, Italy's *Rex* continued in regular service to the Mediterreanean as if totally unaffected by the events in Northern Europe. In the end, the Italian liners proved to be among the final ships trading on a commercial basis. Their sailings ceased in the spring of 1940.

MAINTAINING NEUTRALITY.

In the fall of 1939, the ferocious German Wehrmacht was aiming at its relentless march through France. Hordes of refugees and trapped tourists sought passage, preferrably to America. The United States liners *Manhattan* and *Washington* were still neutral and trying to maintain something of a commercial service. American colors were painted along the sides, on the sun deck and even on the tops of the hatch covers of the *Manhattan (above)*, hopefully warding off prowling enemy subs or bombers. The *Manhattan* and the *Washington* had certificates for 1,200 passengers, but in this desperate time, they often sailed with over 2,000. Four and six shared cabins while others used cots in the public rooms *(right)* and even the bottom of the drained indoor swimming pool. Arturo Toscanini shared the chief surgeon's cabin while cosmetic queen Helena Rubinstein made do with a sofa in the smoking room. [*Manhattan:* Built by New York Shipbuilding Company, Camden, New Jersey, 1932. 24,289 gross tons; 705 feet long; 86 feet wide. Steam turbines geared to twin screw. Service speed 20 knots. 1,239 passengers (582 cabin class, 461 first class, 196 third class).]

The War Years

In the years between 1940 and 1945, a third of the world's liner fleet was destroyed. All but three of the superliners were gone. Modern company terminals and piers, such as those for Holland-America at Rotterdam, were turned to twisted masses of steel.

The Allied war effort at sea was a magnificent feat. By 1941, every passenger ship — from the Cunard *Queens* to small coastal steamers — was in use by the military. Their routes and needs were diverse, often changeable and usually top secret. The *Mauretania* had been to Sydney, the *Ile de France* to Capetown, and the *Queen Elizabeth* to San Francisco. Life in a medium-sized liner converted to trooper was quite different from that on the old glamor runs. With as many as 10,000 servicemen on board, two meals per day — breakfast and dinner — were served in ten sittings of 20 minutes each. Breakfast started at seven. A typical menu featured cereal, boiled eggs, bread and jam, cheese and coffee or tea. Dinner began at 4:30 with thick soup, meat and potatoes or stew, and dessert. The daily consumption was mind-boggling: 240 gallons of milk, 14,000 loaves of bread, 880 pounds of butter, 80 bags of flour.

Both Allied and Axis liners suffered a variety of fates. While most were transformed into troopships, some were converted to aircraft carriers, hospitals, diplomatic exchanges, prisons, repair plants, even floating concentration camps. Fire, torpedoes and aerial bombings were ever-present dangers. Those that survived were sometimes no longer recognizable: funnels and masts were gone, new decks had been built, interiors were completely changed.

At the war's end all of the German liners were either destroyed or seized as prizes. The Japanese had only one passenger ship surviving, an 11,000-tonner. All but four of Italy's superb fleet was in ruins.

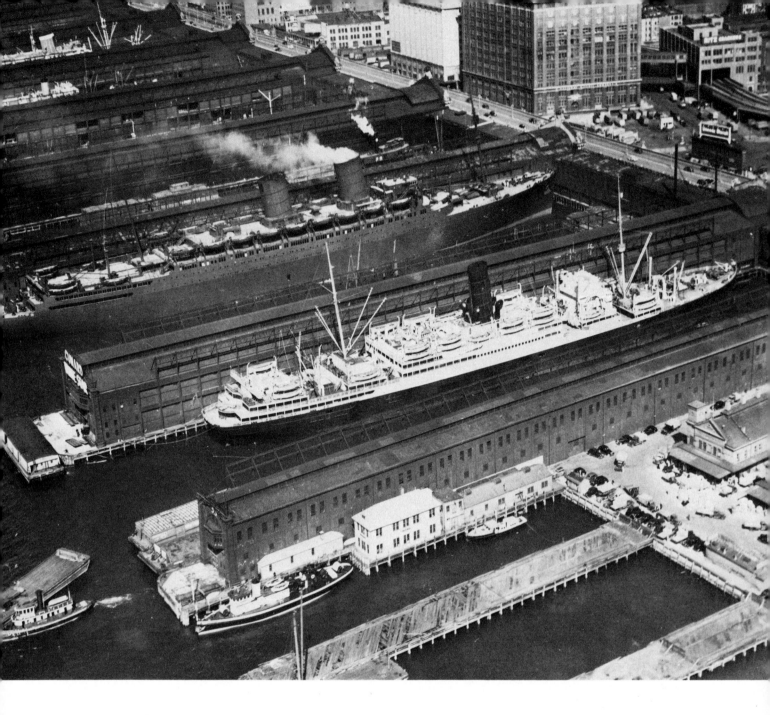

THE SPRING OF 1940.

Many liners remained in safer American waters. Together at piers in Hoboken (opposite, top) Holland-America's West-ernland (top), Nieuw Amsterdam (center) and Volendam (bottom) were either laid-up or resting between short pleasure trips to Bermuda and the Caribbean.

Subsequently, in September, the Nieuw Amsterdam was converted into a troopship (opposite, bottom). Over the next six years, she carried over 378,000 troops, an average of 8,599 per voyage.

The initial task of removing her beautiful public rooms and cabins was done largely by Chinese labor at Singapore. Much of it suffered grievous damage through haste, care-lessness and misuse. Furniture, decorations and carpets re-mained in piles, along the Singapore docks for weeks, in all weather. Later, the furnishings were shipped to Australia

and then to San Francisco before going home to Rotterdam in 1946. Her transformation included the stripping of all C Deck cabins, which were replaced by more than 1,000 ham-mocks. The grand hall became a duplex dormitory for 600 in three-tier standee bunks. The theater slept 386 and each suite held 22.

The scene along New York's Chelsea docks (above) was rapidly showing signs of the coming war. The Cunarder Samaria, at the lower Pier 54, has had her commercial fun-nel colors painted over in black. The Mauretania is already completely in gray and soon to sail on her first military voyage. At the top, the stacks of the United States Lines' Washington retain their peacetime markings, since America was officially still neutral.

STOCKHOLM (above).

The largest Swedish liner yet built, the *Stockholm*, was still under construction when the war started. She was launched at Trieste on March 10, 1940, appearing quite normal in her commercial colors. Shortly afterward, the Italian government seized her and she was finished as the trooper *Sabaudia*. Her brief life ended during an Allied air attack on the port of Trieste in July 1944. [Built by Cantieri Riuniti dell'Adriatico, Monfalcone, Italy, 1941. 29,307 gross tons; 675 feet long; 83 feet wide. Sulzer diesels geared to triple screw. Service speed 19 knots. 1,350 passengers.]

OSLOFJORD (opposite)

Another Scandinavian, the two-year-old Norwegian America *Oslofjord*, fell victim to a magnetic mine in December 1940. [Built by A. G. Weser Shipyards, Bremen, Germany, 1938. 18,673 gross tons; 590 feet long; 73 feet wide. M.A.N. diesels geared to twin screw. Service speed 19.5 knots. 860 passengers (152 cabin class, 307 tourist class, 401 third class).]

ROYAL REFUGEES (above).

The Duke and Duchess of Windsor were evacuated from Europe in the summer of 1940, traveling in American Export's *Excalibur* from Lisbon to a specially arranged stop at Bermuda. The Windsors occupied six connecting cabins, had a private deck area and sailed with over 50 pieces of luggage. Few individuals could claim to have escaped with such style. [Built by New York Shipbuilding Corporation, Camden, New Jersey, 1930. 9,359 gross tons; 474 feet long; 61 feet wide. Steam turbine geared to a single screw. Service speed 16 knots. 125 first-class passengers.]

ILE DE FRANCE (opposite, top).

At the war's outbreak, the *Ile de France* was berthed at her New York pier. Since the French were not anxious to return the ship to its homeland, she was towed to Staten Island by ten tugs and was laid up following special dredging that cost $30,000. Her crew of 800 was reduced to a security staff of 100 while she sat inoperative for the next five months. Then, during March 1940, under the command of the British Admiralty to whom she had been loaned, the *Ile* was loaded with 12,000 tons of war materials, submarine oil, copper ingots, brass bars, shells and several uncrated bombers that were stowed on aft open decks. On May 1, she departed for Europe, veiled in gray and black. From there, she sailed to Singapore where, following the fall of France, she was officially seized by the British.

THE *QUEENS* AS TROOPSHIPS (opposite, bottom).

The *Queen Elizabeth* and the *Queen Mary* (shown here) were, without question, the most outstanding troopships of the war. Churchill claimed that together they helped to shorten the war in Europe by at least a year. Their speed and capacity made them invaluable. Hitler offered an Iron Cross and $250,000 to the U-boat commander who could sink them. Fortunately, they outstepped most warships and worked independently from the customary convoy crossings. In the early part of the war the great pair sailed in the Indian Ocean, ferrying soldiers to the Middle East and Africa from Australia. Returning, they carried prisoners of war, the wounded and evacuees. Although the ships gave sterling service, they lacked adequate air-cooling systems in a climate for which they were never intended. Very often, they were sizzling infernos. In 1943, the two switched to the Atlantic troop shuttle, taking 15,000 from New York to Britain each week, a figure seven times greater than their designed capacities. Careful steps were taken to avoid the possibilities of one of these massive ships capsizing. Equal numbers of troops were contained in separate areas to balance the hulls. The *Mary* established the highest record of all time: 16,683 during a crossing in July 1943. Both ships worked well into 1945.

They were not without their share of mishaps. The *Queen Mary* rammed and sank the British cruiser *Curaçoa* on October 2, 1942, off the Scottish coast. 338 crew members from the warship perished. The *Queen Elizabeth* fared better. During a Pacific trip early in the war, however, she was grounded for several hours in San Francisco Bay, fortunately without serious damages. By the war's end, the *Queens* had carried over two million troops.

QUEEN ELIZABETH.

The world's biggest liner, Cunard's *Queen Elizabeth* (*above*), was still at the shipbuilders when hostilities started — a target for sabotage or Nazi bombers. She was finished in gray, and preparations were made at Southampton for her arrival from Clydebank. Instead, under strict Allied secrecy, she went direct from Scotland to the security of New York. She had sailed in such a haste that some workmen found themselves left aboard. On the dangerous crossing, she had the speed to outrace any Axis warship or submarine that might have spotted her. She docked at New York in March 1940, but without the fanfare that would have been her reception in better times. [Built by John Brown & Company Limited, Clydebank, Scotland, 1940. 83,673 tons; 1,031 feet long; 118 feet wide. Steam turbines geared to quadruple screw. Service speed 28.5 knots. 2,283 passengers (823 first class, 662 cabin class, 798 tourist class, 11,027 troops during wartime).]

In the spring of 1940, for a brief period at New York's Piers 88 and 90 (*opposite*) the *Queen Elizabeth* (right) and the *Normandie* (left), the two mightiest liners ever built, were berthed together.

THE DESTRUCTION
OF THE *NORMANDIE*.

The *Normandie* had been scheduled to be at sea, bound for Europe, when Poland was invaded on September 1, 1939. The American Coast Guard, fearful that munitions moved abroad in foreign liners, delayed her sailing for several days of more thorough inspections. As the war reached more serious proportions, it seemed the best course to keep the *Normandie* in New York. When France fell in the following year, she was still idle at Manhattan's Pier 88. Her crew had been reduced to a bare 110. Proposals suggested rebuilding her as an aircraft carrier, gutting her vast interiors. Finally, on May 15, 1941, she was seized by the U.S. Government. Seven months later, she was transferred to the Navy and renamed U.S.S. *Lafayette*, the war's second-largest troopship. Shipyard crews invaded the great ship, removing the sumptuous fittings, and preparing her for military duty. On February 9, 1942, sparks from an acetylene torch ignited a group of life jackets and mattresses. The fire spread quickly.

SALVAGING THE *NORMANDIE* (opposite).
Although the fire destroyed a good portion of the *Normandie's* inner parts, her total destruction was the result of fire-fighting methods. Numerous tugs, fireboats and land equipment poured tons of water onto the blistering hull. She was unable to withstand the pressure and capsized within 12 hours. On her side *(top)*, the *Normandie* presented the most difficult salvage job in history.

On October 27, 1943, after 20 months, the *Normandie* was righted. The process involved removing the masts, the three funnels and all of the superstructure *(bottom)*. The complete project, although used for important Navy diving training, cost $5 million. Laid up for a time, the ship was declared surplus in 1945 and later sold to a local scrapper for a mere $161,000.

WESTERNLAND (above).
After the fall of Holland in May 1940, the seat of the exiled Dutch Government was moved to the troopship *Westernland,* anchored off Falmouth, England. For two months she was the headquarters for 800 officials under the direction of Prince Bernhard, the husband of Crown Princess Juliana. [Built by Harland & Wolff Limited, Belfast, Northern Ireland, 1918. 16,314 gross tons; 601 feet long; 67 feet wide. Steam triple expansion engines geared to triple screw. Service speed 15 knots. 1,500 passengers (350 cabin class, 350 tourist class, 800 third class).]

VOLENDAM *(opposite, top).*
Holland-America's *Volendam* was assigned to the scheme to evacuate children from Britain to the United States and Canada in the summer months of 1940. On August 30, with 335 children and 271 adult passengers aboard, she was torpedoed 300 miles off the Irish coast. Sinking by the bow, the passengers and crew left the liner, miraculously with the loss of only one life. *Volendam's* bow was awash, with the ship drawing 54 feet of water. She was taken in tow and brought to the Isle of Bute. Temporary repairs were made before she was taken to a Birkenhead shipyard for more thorough patching. At the shipyard, a second torpedo was found embedded in the hull. It had obviously failed to explode on contact. [Built by Harland & Wolff Limited, Govan, Scotland, 1922. 15,434 gross tons; 579 feet long; 67 feet wide. Steam turbines geared to twin screw. Service speed 15 knots. 1,175 passengers (263 first class, 428 second class, 484 tourist class).]

TROOP TRANSPORT.
Waiting berths *(opposite, bottom),* were photographed aboard the former Ward Line cruiseship *Oriente,* which by 1942 had become the U.S. Army transport *Thomas H. Barry.* The ship held 530 passengers in peacetime but had a troop capacity of 3,609 during the war.

With life jackets in place, over 4,000 troops *(above)* are aboard the *Britannic* for an Atlantic crossing in 1942.

WARTIME SINKINGS.

On November 2, 1942, while on a voyage from South Africa to New York, Holland-America's *Zaandam (opposite, top)* was struck by two Nazi torpedoes 400 miles off the Brazilian coast. She sank within 10 minutes. There were 124 casualties. An American Navy vessel rescued three survivors 82 days later. Their endurance against the open seas was the greatest on record. [Built by Wilton-Fijenoord Shipyards, Schiedam, Holland, 1938. 10,909 gross tons; 501 feet long; 64 feet wide. M.A.N. diesels geared to twin screw. Service speed 17 knots. 160 tourist-class passengers.]

With 5,000 troops aboard, the transport *President Coolidge (opposite, bottom)* struck a mine off Noumea, New Caledonia, in October 1942, and quickly sank. Five perished.

P & O's *Strathallan (above)*, loaded with a large number of troops and some of General Eisenhower's immediate staff, was torpedoed on December 21, 1942, while on a voyage from England to North Africa. Four passengers died. During the war it was not unusual to have 15 to 20 ships sunk in a single day. [Built by Vickers Armstrongs Shipbuilders Limited, Barrow-in-Furness, England, 1938. 23,722 gross tons; 668 feet long; 82 feet wide. Steam turbines geared to twin screw. Service speed 20 knots. 5,000 troops.]

MONTEREY *(over)*.

The former Pacific cruise liner *Monterey* rests in dry dock in Brooklyn, in September 1942. The ship had a peacetime capacity of 701 passengers. Although the wartime certificate was for 3,851, that number was often exceeded. [Built by Bethlehem Shipbuilding Corporation, Quincy, Massachusetts, 1932. 18,017 gross tons; 632 feet long; 79 feet wide. Steam turbines geared to twin screw. Service speed 20.5 knots. 3,851 troops.]

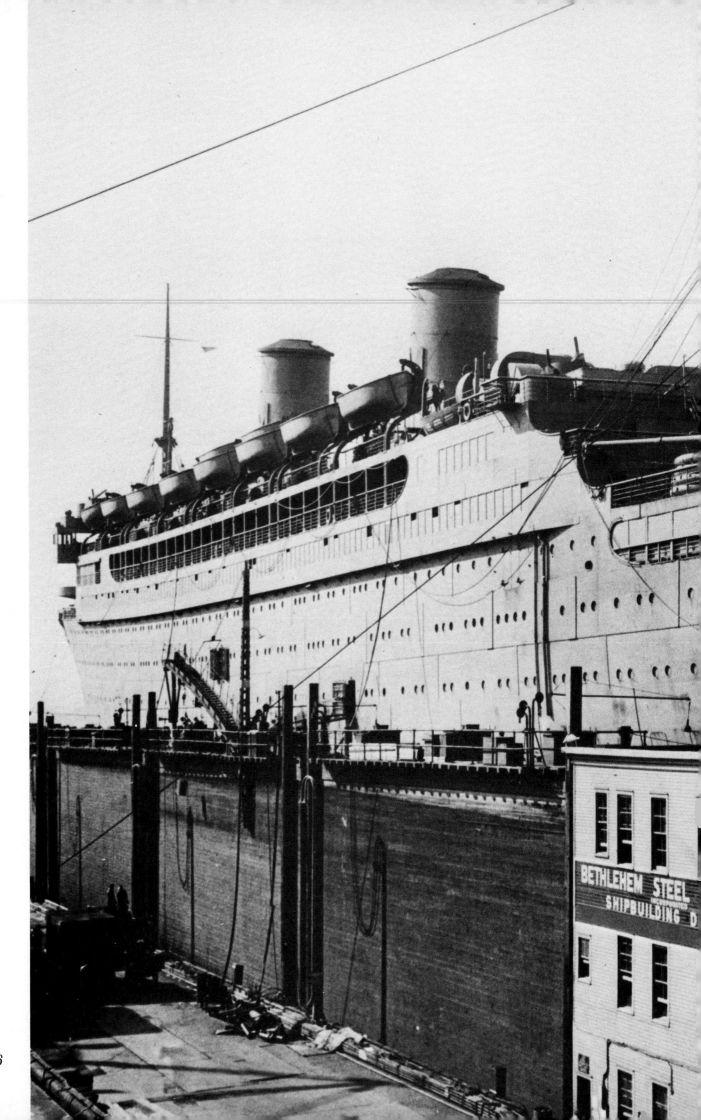

ETHLEHEM STEEL COMPANY
INCORPORATED
SHIPBUILDING DIVISION

WILHELM GUSTLOFF (*opposite, top*).
The former German luxury cruise ship *Wilhelm Gustloff* was turned into a floating concentration camp early in 1945. As the war turned against the Nazis, she attempted a dash into the Baltic while heavily loaded. She was torpedoed and quickly sank in icy waters. An estimated 6,096 perished—the worst maritime catastrophe in history. Built by Blohm & Voss Shipyards, Hamburg, Germany, 1938. 25,484 gross tons; 684 feet long; 77 feet wide. M.A.N. diesels geared to twin screw. Service speed 15.5 knots. 1,465 tourist-class passengers.]

ANCON (*opposite, bottom*).
Panama Line's *Ancon*, flying the Stars and Stripes, was restyled for a time as a communications ship. She was one of the first Allied ships to steam into Tokyo Bay in August 1945. Wedged between Halsey's battleship *Missouri* and Nimitz's *South Dakota*, the former liner played host to over 150 war correspondents, photographers and newsreel technicians. From her decks came the news of the Japanese surrender. [Built by Bethlehem Steel Company, Quincy, Massachusetts, 1939. 10,021 gross tons; 493 feet long; 64 feet wide; 26-foot draft. Steam turbines geared to twin screw. Service speed 17.5 knots. 215 peacetime first-class passengers. 2,087 troops in wartime.]

RETURNING TROOPS (*above*).
By the late spring of 1945, the fighting in Europe was over. The *Queen Mary* arrived in New York harbor on June 20 with the first shipload of returning soldiers, 14,777 in all.

A WELCOME HOME.

The American Export Lines repainted the far end of their Jersey City pier in New York harbor as part of the homecoming celebrations. Many joyous moments occurred at these piers. The *Gripsholm*, shown in the photograph, had just landed over 1,000 refugees. Across the Hudson, the United Fruit piers had a sign that thanked returning troops for "a job well done." Indeed it was. [Built by Armstrong Whitworth & Company Limited, Newcastle-upon-Tyne, England, 1925. 19,105 gross tons; 590 feet long; 74 feet wide. Burmeister & Wain diesels geared to twin screw. Service speed 16 knots. 1,557 peacetime passengers.]

The Postwar Period

In the summer of 1945, liner companies took immediate steps toward revitalizing the old commercial trades. Sadly, however, they had fewer ships than before. Therefore, orders of the day were twofold: refitting and rebuilding the survivors, and creating new tonnage.

Many of the troopships were released from military duty at slower rates than expected, some not until 1950. A few were never returned to the luxury business. The remainders went off to the shipyards, often their original builders, for the great transformation to peacetime use. Frequently, it was a long and difficult process. Supplies and materials were in staggering shortages, particularly in Europe. Shipyards were vastly overcrowded. Sometimes there was an additional delay. A troopship refitting at Glasgow might have to wait for furniture and other fixtures, which might have been hurriedly dumped ashore at a point as remote as Singapore in 1939. The postwar transshipment was sometimes incredibly slow.

Over a dozen brand-new liners appeared between 1948 and 1954. America produced the most brilliant of all — the speedy *United States* — in 1952.

Rather quickly, the commercial trades settled back into prosperity. Tourist services resumed, and there were vast numbers of refugees, immigrants and repatriates in need of ships. By 1948, for example, the North Atlantic run was beginning its most profitable decade in history.

EUROPA — A PRIZE OF WAR (over).
In May of 1945, American invasion forces raced for the German port of Bremerhaven. The prize was the then third-largest liner in the world, North German Lloyd's *Europa*. Upon boarding, the troops found little of her prewar elegance. She had been rusting and ill-kept since being laid up in September 1939. Yellowing boarding signs had been posted for Nazi troops that had never come aboard. Huge doors had been cut into her sides for the intended invasion of Britain. But she had never been used. At the war's end, an order came from Berlin to destroy the ship. It was disobeyed. The prewar commander and his small crew offered their services to the Allies. The ship was quickly designated AP-177, the U.S.S. *Europa*. In mid-September, after a brief cleaning and paint job, she steamed off to New York with 4,300 troops and 960 crew aboard. She was at sea for the first time in six years. After a refitting at New York, the *Europa* made a few hurried trooping voyages. But she was plagued by a series of fires, one of which lasted nine hours. On another day, five had to be extinguished. Then, just to complicate matters, some serious hull cracking was uncovered. Although very much in need of repair she was handed over to the United Nations Reparations Commission in February of 1946. Here she is seen next to the U.S.S. *Missouri*.

EUROPA BECOMES THE LIBERTE.

The loss of the *Normandie* gave the French the strongest claim to the *Europa*, so the ship hoisted the tricolor. The new name chosen for her was the *Lorraine*, but in the great outpouring of feeling at the war's end, *Liberté* seemed more fitting. The first step was to paint the funnels in French Line red and black. Then she docked at Le Havre for the long rebuilding for luxury service. Because of shortages, work progressed at a snail's pace. A December gale tore the *Liberté* from her moorings and threw her into the half-submerged wreck of the prewar liner *Paris*, creating a 30-foot gash. She settled quickly, but fortunately in an upright position *(above)*. The restoration work stopped as salvage took priority. Six months later, she was refloated and by spring 1947 was at St. Nazaire for the final rebuilding.

The French Line's new flagship *Liberté* arrived in New York for the first time in August 1950 *(opposite, top)*. She had been through three years of amputations, transplants and face-lifting. The Germanic profile remained but the French produced a magnificent Art Deco interior. Looking at the ship's columned main lounge *(opposite, bottom)*, it was difficult to remember the trials she had endured. [Built by Blohm & Voss Shipyards, Hamburg, Germany, 1930. 51,839 gross tons; 936 feet long; 102 feet wide. Steam turbines geared to quadruple screw. Service speed 27 knots. 1,513 passengers (569 first class, 562 cabin class, 382 tourist class).]

STAVANGERFJORD (opposite).

Idle and unharmed during the war, Norwegian America Line's *Stavangerfjord* made the first commercial sailing, in August 1945, on the North Atlantic. [Built by Cammell Laird & Company, Birkenhead, England, 1918. 13,156 gross tons; 553 feet long; 64 feet wide. Steam turbines geared to twin screw. Service speed 18 knots. 679 passengers (122 first class, 222 cabin class, 335 tourist class).]

THE RETURN OF THE *QUEENS* (above).

To the British, one of the greatest signs of "peace at last" was the return of the mighty Cunard *Queens*. The *Queen Elizabeth* was released first. She was quickly turned into the luxury ship that was originally planned in 1940. On

September 27, 1946, the *Queen Mary* (right) steamed into Southampton, returning from her final military voyage and passing the nearly complete *Queen Elizabeth*. The restoration had been a staggering project. Warehouses in both Britain and America had to be unloaded and the contents shipped to the Clydebank, Scotland shipyards. Labor was so hard-pressed that additional help came from France. Finally, on July 31, 1947, the *Queen Mary* joined her running-mate and began the two-ship Cunard weekly express service. It was the first time in Cunard history that weekly departures could be made in each direction by two liners. As a result, their success was brilliant. For the next decade, they were the most profitable pair on the Atlantic.

REFITTING THE *NIEUW AMSTERDAM* (opposite, top).
The *Nieuw Amsterdam* triumphantly returned to her home port of Rotterdam on April 10, 1946. Fifteen weeks were required to remove the troop fittings: the special kitchens, alarm systems, hammocks, standees and the 36 guns. Then 2,000 tons of furniture and decorations were shipped to Holland from wartime storage in San Francisco. The furnishings were often in very poor condition, a result of six years of neglect. About 3,000 chairs and 500 tables were sent back to their original builders for reupholstering and refinishing. One quarter of the furnishings had to be replaced entirely. Factories and warehouses in Europe combed their supplies of materials and fabrics, much of which had been concealed from the Nazis during the occupation. Many smaller parts, such as hinges and clamps, had to be made by hand, the machinery that once made them having been stolen or destroyed by the enemy. The entire rubber flooring was renewed, as was nearly all of the carpeting. All of the steel work was scaled and preserved and all piping cleaned. All ceilings and floors were removed; all of the liner's 374 bathrooms were rebuilt. In the passenger spaces, the wood paneling, which had been scratched and mutilated, was planed down to half its thickness and relacquered. All the cabins' closets and fixtures were replaced. The entire electrical wiring system was renewed. Having been painted over for blackouts and cracked in tropical climates, 12,000 square feet of glass was refurbished. Even the handrails had to be repolished to eradicate thousands of carved initials. The project was monumental, because of the material shortages and the decline of the number of skilled craftsmen. On October 29, 1947, after 18 months at the shipyards, the *Nieuw Amsterdam* reentered transatlantic service. Over 100 liners were restored with similar efforts.

STOCKHOLM (opposite, bottom).
The motorliner *Stockholm* of the Swedish American Line was the first new passenger ship built for the North Atlantic run following the war. Her keel plates were laid down in 1946 and she crossed to New York on her maiden voyage in the winter of 1948. [Built by Gotaverken Shipyards, Gothenburg, Sweden, 1948. 11,700 gross tons; 525 feet long; 68 feet wide. Gotaverken diesels geared to twin screw. Service speed 19 knots. 395 passengers (113 first class, 282 tourist class).]

CARONIA (above).
The Cunard Line conceived of the *Caronia* in 1948. She was Britain's biggest postwar liner and Princess Elizabeth (today the Queen) traveled to Scotland for the launching ceremony. But there were other novelties: She was dual purpose, running transatlantic crossings only in the peak summer months and spending the remainder of the year on long, expensive cruises. The hull was painted in four shades of green, supposedly for heat resistance and easy identification. She had the greatest single mast and the largest stack afloat. Finally, and just for good measure, every cabin had a private adjoining bathroom—a far cry from all previous Cunarders. Affectionately known as the "Green Goddess," the *Caronia* was also called the "millionaire's ship." Her exotic pattern remained much the same: in winter, around the world or the South Seas; in spring, the Mediterreanean and Black Seas; in summer, Scandinavia; and in fall, the Mediterranean again. [Built by John Brown & Company Limited, Clydebank, Scotland, 1948. 34,183 gross tons; 715 feet long; 91 feet wide. Steam turbines geared to twin screw. Service speed 22 knots. 932 passengers (581 first class, 351 cabin class).]

ORONTES (above).

Britain's Orient Line had lost four liners, each over 20,000 tons, during the war years. Refits and rebuilding were therefore immediate orders of business to reestablish the busy Australian passenger trade. The *Orontes*, dating from 1929 and fortunate enough to have survived the war, had a $2.5 million refurbishing after military duty. Shipyard costs were rising rapidly. She had been built less than 20 years before for the same amount. [Built by Vickers Armstrongs Shipbuilders Limited, Barrow-in-Furness, England, 1929. 20,186 gross tons; 664 feet long; 75 feet wide. Steam turbines geared to twin screw. Service speed 20 knots. 1,112 passengers (502 first class, 610 tourist class).]

ORCADES (opposite, top).

The *Orcades* was the first of the new postwar liners built for the Orient Line. She was completed in December 1948.

Costing $9 million, she was distinctive in being the first passenger ship to group her funnel and mast above the bridge so closely. Her speed cut the sailing time from London to Melbourne to 26 days, ten less than the previous standard. [Built by Vickers Armstrongs Shipbuilders Limited, Barrow-in-Furness, England, 1948. 28,164 gross tons; 709 feet long; 90 feet wide. Steam turbines geared to twin screw. Service speed 22 knots. 1,545 passengers (773 first class, 774 tourist class).]

HIMALAYA (opposite, bottom).

Soft chairs, comfortable sofas and card tables filled out the tourist-class main lounge aboard the British *Himalaya* of P&O Lines. The arrangement dates from 1949.

P. & O. HIMALAYA TOURIST LOUNGE

ORONSAY *(above)*.
The simple attractive tourist-class restaurant of the Orient Line's *Oronsay*, 1951.

PRESIDENT WILSON (opposite).
The passenger run on the Pacific did not revive as quickly as that on the Atlantic. However, American President Lines of San Francisco took a great step in 1947–48 by commissioning the sister ships *President Cleveland* and *President Wilson (top)*. The pair reopened something of the prewar service: from San Francisco to Honolulu, Yokohama, Kobe, Hong Kong and Manila. [Built by Bethlehem Alameda Shipyard, Alameda, California, 1948. 15,359 gross tons; 609 feet long; 75 feet wide. Steam turboelectric engines geared to twin screw. Service speed 19 knots. 778 passengers (324 first class, 454 tourist class).]

A view of the sitting room in a first-class suite *(bottom)* reflects the trend to greater simplicity in design and decoration.

RETURN OF THE *ILE DE FRANCE (over)*.
In the autumn of 1945, the *Ile de France* was returned to the French Line after five years of outstanding military service with the British Admiralty. In honor of her wartime performance, British Rail named one of its locomotives *Compagnie Générale Transatlantique*. At first the *Ile* made austerity trips to Canada and Indochina. Then, in April 1947, she went to her builders' yard at St. Nazaire for a two-year restoration. The outcome included the removal of her third, "dummy," stack. She sailed into New York on her first postwar luxury crossing in July 1949. [Built by Chantiers de l'Atlantique, St. Nazaire, France, 1927. 44,356 gross tons; 791 feet long; 91 feet wide. Steam turbines geared to quadruple screw. Service speed 23.5 knots. 1,345 passengers (541 first class, 577 cabin class, 227 tourist class).]

BATORY.

Beginning in May 1949 and lasting through January 1951, the *Batory* of the Polish Ocean Lines was the subject of a series of political incidents. The most serious was the accusation that an alleged spy had escaped from New York aboard her. The situation climaxed when American stevedores and repairmen refused to handle the ship. The *Batory* had to be withdrawn and was rerouted on a new service from Poland to India and Pakistan via the Suez Canal. [Built by Cantieri Riuniti dell'Adriatico, Monfalcone, Italy, 1936. 14,287 gross tons; 526 feet long; 70 feet wide. Sulzer diesels geared to twin screw. Service speed 18 knots. 832 passengers (412 first class, 420 tourist class).]

AMERICA.

It took $6 million to refurbish United States Lines' *America* following six years of strenuous war service. [Built by Newport News Shipbuilding & Drydock Company, Newport News, Virginia, 1940. 33,961 gross tons; 723 feet long; 94 feet wide. Steam turbines geared to twin screw. Service speed 22.5 knots. 1,046 passengers (516 first class, 530 tourist class).]

The *America*. Elegance and luxury returned to sea in the postwar era. A first-class suite de luxe *(opposite, top)* was decorated in quiet, restrained taste. The main ballroom *(opposite, bottom)* had a circular dance floor illuminated by indirect lighting. The first-class restaurant *(above)* was all shine and sleekness.

SATURNIA (opposite, top).
The Italian Line's *Saturnia* is viewed from her running-mate *Vulcania* in 1949. The ships were two of Italy's four major liners to survive the war, the others being the *Conte Biancamano* and the *Conte Grande*. [Built by Cantieri Navale Triestino, Monfalcone, Italy, 1927. 24,346 gross tons; 632 feet long; 79 feet wide. Sulzer diesels geared to twin screw. Service speed 21 knots. 1,370 passengers (240 first class, 270 cabin class, 860 tourist class).]

CONTE BIANCAMANO (opposite, bottom).
The first-class Gallery in the Italian Line's *Conte Biancamano* is seen followng her 1948–49 postwar refit. The ship dated from 1925.

GIULIO CESARE (above).
The company directors of the Italian Line, faced with rebuilding, thought that superliners were wasteful symbols of a bygone era. Therefore, building blueprints called for nothing larger than 30,000 tons. The *Giulio Cesare*—photographed at the fitting-out berth at Monfalcone—entered the Italian service to Rio de Janeiro, Montevideo and Buenos Aires in October 1951. [Built by Cantieri Riuniti dell'Adriatico, Monfalcone, Italy, 1951. 27,078 gross tons; 681 feet long; 87 feet wide. Fiat diesels geared to twin screw. Service speed 21 knots. 1,180 passengers (178 first class, 288 cabin class, 714 tourist class).]

CRISTOFORO COLOMBO.
For the fancier New York trade, the Italian Line built the sisterships *Andrea Doria* and *Cristoforo Colombo*. They were more ornate and spacious, and among the finest modern liners on the North Atlantic in the fifties. When the *Cristoforo Colombo* arrived at New York on her maiden voyage in July 1954, she signaled the completion of the post-war rebirth of Italy's passenger fleet of 11 new passenger ships. [Built by Ansaldo Shipyards, Genoa, Italy, 1954. 29,191 gross tons; 700 feet long; 90 feet wide. 1,055 passengers (229 first class, 222 cabin class, 604 tourist class).]

THE END OF THE *GEORGE WASHINGTON* (*above*).
One old American liner, the *George Washington*, burned at
Baltimore in January 1951. The loss of ship and pier
amounted to $20 million. [Built by A. G. Vulcan Shipyard,
Stettin, Germany, 1908. 23,788 gross tons; 722 feet long; 78
feet wide; 30-foot draft. Steam quadruple expansion engines
geared to twin screw. Service speed 18.5 knots. 6,500
troops.]

INDEPENDENCE (*over*).
On a brighter note, $20 million brought out the *Indepen-
dence* for American Export Lines in the same year. [Built by
Bethlehem Steel Company, Quincy, Massachusetts, 1951.
23,719 gross tons; 683 feet long; 89 feet wide; 30-foot draft.
Steam turbines geared to twin screw. Service speed 23
knots. 1,000 passengers (295 first class, 375 cabin class, 330
tourist class).]

MAASDAM *(above, top).*

The *Ryndam* and *Maasdam* (shown here) were notable additions to the "Atlantic Ferry" in 1951–52. Their design introduced tourist-class dominance of the accommodations. First-class space, with a mere 39 berths, was arranged in an exclusive penthouse section on the upper decks. It had a separate restaurant and public rooms. The tourist-class section, which occupied 90 percent of the ship's passenger spaces, had staterooms for 822 passengers. There were also several public rooms, a large dining salon, an outdoor swimming pool and considerable open-air deck areas. These berths, although quite modern and comfortable, were offered at inexpensive rates, averaging $20 per day. [Built by Wilton-Fijenoord Shipyward, Schiedam, Holland, 1952. 15,024 gross tons; 503 feet long; 69 feet wide. Steam turbines geared to single screw. Service speed 16.5 knots. 861 passengers (39 first class, 822 tourist class).]

FLANDRE *(above, bottom).*

The French Line's first new postwar liner, the smart-looking *Flandre*, left Le Havre on her maiden voyage to New York on July 23, 1952. When nearing the American Coast, she was abruptly immobilized by mechanical and electrical failures. Without power, the *Flandre* gained the dubious distinction of being the only passenger ship towed into port on her first trip, and was quickly dubbed "the Flounder" by stevedores. Later she was sent back to her builders for repairs that kept her off the Atlantic for nine months. [Built by Ateliers et Chantiers de France, Dunkirk, France, 1952. 20,469 gross tons; 600 feet long; 80 feet wide. Steam turbines geared to twin screw. Service speed 22 knots. 784 passengers (402 first class, 285 cabin class, 97 tourist class).]

UNITED STATES.

As early as 1943, America's foremost marine designer, William Francis Gibbs, began drawings for a supership that would be the fastest and safest ever built. The U.S. Government gave its support, realizing such a ship's value as a possible troopship, especially after the blazing success of the Cunard *Queens* during the war. By the late forties, the final plans had been completed under the tightest security. The keel was laid down in February 1950, and work progressed through day and night shifts. She was floated out (not traditionally launched) when 90 percent complete, little more than 15 months later. The new greyhound was outstandingly modern: a long, slender hull with a brief mast above the bridge and two raked, massive funnels. Although a mere 40 feet shorter than the *Queen Elizabeth*, the American flagship was 30,000 tons lighter, because of the use of aluminum alloys. Her naming ceremony was a rather simple affair, unlike the royal or celebrity launches given to most of the European superliners. The name *United States* seemed a most appropriate choice. [Built by Newport News Shipbuilding & Drydock Company, Newport News, Virginia, 1952. 53,329 gross tons; 990 feet long; 101 feet wide. Steam turbines geared to quadruple screw. Service speed 30–33 knots. 1,928 passengers (871 first class, 508 cabin class, 549 tourist class).]

The *United States*. The ship was fitted out at Newport News early in 1952 *(above)*.

Her interiors, such as a cabin *(left)*, displayed functional, less opulent, luxury. Safety, particularly against fire, was the ruling force: no wood except in the pianos and butchers' blocks, no flammable materials, not even in the oil paintings. The government sponsors, which paid three-quarters of the $77 million cost, were more than pleased with the ship, especially because she could be transformed in 48 hours to handle 15,000 troops.

A head-on view *(opposite)* reveals the knife-like prow of the ship.

By the late spring of 1952, she was ready. Her statistics were still a well-guarded secret. The sea trials were brilliantly successful; it was revealed much later that she had exceeded 40 knots, making her by far the fastest passenger ship ever built. The "Big U," as she was fondly known, was given a spectacular reception at New York *(over)*. During her maiden voyage to Southampton, in July 1952, she immediately captured the Blue Ribbon, running 5 knots and 10 hours faster than the *Queen Mary's* best run. The *United States* averaged 35 knots. No luxury ship will ever outpace her.

Bibliography

Bonsor, N. R. P.: *North Atlantic Seaway*, Prescot, Lancashire, 1955.

Braynard, Frank O.: *Lives of the Liners*, New York, 1947.

Brinnin, John Malcolm: *The Sway of the Grand Saloon*, New York, 1971.

Buchanan, Lamont: *Ships of Steam*, New York, 1956.

Cairis, Nicholas T.: *North Atlantic Passenger Liners Since 1900*, London, 1972.

Coleman, Terry: *The Liners*, New York, 1977.

Cronican, Frank and Mueller, Edward A.: *The Stateliest Ship*, New York, 1968.

Crowdy, Michael (editor): *Marine News* (World Ship Society journal), Kendal, Cumbria, 1964–1979.

Dunn Laurence: *Passenger Liners*, Southampton, 1961.

Eisele, Peter: *Steamboat Bill* (Steamship Historical Society of America journal), New York, 1966–1979.

Gibbs, C. R. Vernon: *British Passenger Liners of the Five Oceans*, London, 1963.

Kludas, Arnold: *Great Passenger Ships of the World*, Volumes 1–5, Cambridge, 1972–1974.

Maxtone-Graham, John: *The Only Way to Cross*, New York, 1972.

Mitchell, Alan: *Splendid Sisters*, London, 1966.

Moscow, Alvin: *Collision Course*, New York, 1959.

Seabrook, William C.: *In the War at Sea*, New York, 1947.

Smith, Eugene W.: *Passenger Ships of the World Past and Present*, Boston, 1963.

Wall, Robert: *Ocean Liners*, New York, 1977.

Index